Up The Creek With Old Harry

Another collection of the 'Old Harry' stories
originally published in *Yachts and Yachting*
and *Yachting Monthly*

written and illustrated by J. D. Sleightholme

D1635854

ADLARD COLES LIMITED
GRANADA PUBLISHING
London Toronto Sydney New York

Published by Granada Publishing in
Adlard Coles Limited, 1979

Granada Publishing Limited
Frogmore, St Albans, Herts AL2 2NF
and
3 Upper James Street, London W1R 4BP
Suite 405, 4th Floor, United Nations Plaza, New York,
NY 10017, USA
Q164 Queen Victoria Buildings, Sydney, NSW 2000, Australia
100 Skyway Avenue, Toronto, Ontario, M9W 3A6, Canada
PO Box 84165, Greenside, 2034 Johannesburg, South Africa
CML Centre, Queen and Wyndham, Auckland 1, New Zealand

Copyright © 1979 by J. D. Sleightholme

ISBN 0 229 11639 6

Set, printed and bound in Great Britain by
Cox & Wyman Ltd, Reading

Granada ®

Also by J. D. Sleightholme

Old Harry's Bunkside Book
Cruising: A Manual for the Small Sailing Boat Owner
Fitting Out: Maintenance and Repair of Small Craft

Contents

Odd Aspects

Introduction

I BEGAN WRITING ABOUT Old Harry over twenty years ago when I was on the staff of *Yachts and Yachting*, continued through leanish years as a freelance and on into my latter times with *Yachting Monthly*. I am grateful both to Peter Cook, editor of the former and to the publishers of the latter (IPC Magazines Ltd) for permission to make this second collection of pieces – a turn of phrase which smacks of brisk work with shovel and sack.

I have not presumed to bring them up to date, and must confess to a sense of furtive relief that any attempt to do so could only be to their detriment. Old Harry himself, for long thought to be without any of the finer feelings, was actually seen to be shyly proud of his *Bunkside Book*, published last year, and only some smart work on the part of his publishers prevented his active co-operation in the preparation of this volume.

The Social Scene

ONE TENDS TO SPEAK OF *'The Yachtsman'* as if he were a separate genetic type, a curious mutant that escaped the biochemist's lab via a dangling necktie in a dish of culture. In fact he is a human being, efficiently disguised. No chiropodist, out of sorts and viewing the first foot of the day with squeamish dislike, can be more aware of the variety than your social hostess lumbered with a mixed bag of yachtsmen on Lifeboat Day.

What really worried the hell out of me recently was the reader of these pieces – an English tutor – who had computer analysed my themes in search of motivation. He traced every sort of influence from Chaucer (probably) to Wodehouse via the British Rail menu. The conception of me as a shrewd student of human nature revealing the foibles of mankind, disguised as humour, for the sharper-eyed to spot ('Look, look, there goes a foible') is quite wrong. I don't even like us all that much.

A test to the ghosts

... and the stampede of women

Every year about this time some hundreds of social (Hon) secretaries are smashing a fist into one of their other hands and saying:

'By the living Harry, I've got it!' (They've probably had it for years.)

They then write out a menu for the club dinner which is so witty that they collapse gnawing the woodwork and screaming with mirth.

Biting our lips and sobbing for breath, we read:

'Tra-peas Soup, Cabin Sole, Poulet Hauly (with greens) and Ices Various.' They cross this out and put 'Glacé calm'. They are carried off on a hurdle.

This business of the Annual Dinner marks the apex of the Yachting Year. It has become a fine art. They have even invented special tables with one leg to each 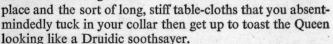 place and the sort of long, stiff table-cloths that you absent-mindedly tuck in your collar then get up to toast the Queen looking like a Druidic soothsayer.

Presiding over-all is the Top Table. The Commodore radiates glory, reflected on a diminishing scale by his neighbours which, as distance increases, becomes less and less until you come to Old Harry near the exit, trying to flick jelly off his lap under the eye of the Head Waiter. Unskilfully done, this arrangement is like a gas fire in a surgery with all the Old Soldiers hogging Punch and singeing their fustian, while a chronic throat and a poisoned thumb shudder in the draught.

A feature of these larks is the stampede of waitresses. This is a carefully rehearsed and morale-wrecking trick aimed at taking the bone out of non-tipping diners. The Head Waiter claps his hand joylessly. Instantly a wall of women pours out from behind curtains, palms and coat racks, like a curse of Egypt, a wobbling tide of black and white thundering out to war.

There have been men whose nerves cracked. I once helped get a small, bald bachelor down from a chandelier. There was the case of the old flag officer who woke with a start . . .

'To me men!' he shouted, leaping on to the table. 'Back you savage devils – they shall not have the flag, boys!'

He went down on one knee and tried to form a British Square but fell in the gravy boat instead.

You must sit firm and sway to the left as they approach. Some waitresses sew razor blades to their cuffs, others favour the smart flick of an elbow.

To be a guest is no easy matter. They place you beside hearty Miss Marlene Spike who has a high Points Total and gums. She doesn't know what you are talking about and drinks out of the wrong glass. The real threat comes with the toasts. The Chairman pounds the table and there is silence save for someone who is left saying . . .

'I find I get it with sprouts . . .'

A white-faced man gets up and announces a 'Test to our ghosts'. All members leap loyally to their feet and give a convincing display of drinking, from empty glasses. You were up before the horror of it struck you. Slowly you lurch down again, like a Church Hall ballerina doing a shot-down swan. As a result of this you are going to remain immovably seated when the guests rise to host their toasts. You feel as if you were at the bottom of a well with a towering, hissing wife looking down on you.

There is the foreign guest who staggers to his feet at the Top Table, unbowed by a succession of terrifying dishes, and tells a foreign joke without a point (due to translation). He is clapped uproariously and protectively, and sits down wondering just what in hell was funny.

After that it becomes confusing. There are cigars, and someone with a scarlet face at the end of the table, whom you never saw before, buys you one. He looks unsteady. You sit there with that great thing stuck in your face looking like a nightmare toucan in a bow tie. You find that you have bought brandies for everyone in sight and you two-finger through your wallet smiling mirthlessly with the wine waiter breathing in your ear.

9

No harm in looking

– but where was the traditional gear – the Stockholm tar and deadeyes?

We went round and round that show like a clockwork train until Harry got trouble with his iodine socks. They balled up in his gumboots so that he walked with the plodding portentousness of a Cinerama Moses coming down a mountain.

There were chairs on somebody's stand, but the moment we sat down in that crowd we got trouble. I got an earful of lolly sticks and a did-it-himself man with turn-ups full of sawdust looked at Harry in his enormous black oily and wanted to know if he was self-inflating. It would have taken a brave man to bend down and tie his shoelace in that maritime mêlée.

We were enjoying it, however, although old Harry was having trouble with his shopping list. He wanted two leather clacks, a wick for his Rippingill, a sheer-pole, four ram's-horns, a rawhide-covered gaff saddle, a set of four-inch dead-eyes and a dolphin striker. He'd already returned a runabout sidelight because there was no flint in it and I'd had to stop him trying to buy the junk that was coming through a bilge pump demonstration.

A stand attendant came at us with his 'good-shoppe' smile and rubbing his hands as if he was trying to work up a lather in cloakroom liquid soap. He saw Harry getting the turns out of his sock and sheered off to tackle a man with Dundreary whiskers and a deerstalker hat, eating egg and tomato sandwiches. With him was a powerful woman in a windcheater, settling herself in a chair like an old broody taking a dust bath.

Sit on a stand long enough and you see all types. There's the character in a bowler and shorty overcoat, with eight pounds fifty in the bank and a thoughtful frown, who brings down a covey of stand attendants as if he'd blown a horn every time he stops to look at a boat. Those men on the stands merit admiration, too. They can side-swipe small boys pinching pamphlets with one hand and fend off inventors with the other and not miss a beat. They may have visitors galloping up and down their ladders like toy firemen, working their handles, picking their floral frontages and digging at their plastic with nail-files, but they can still manage a jolly word for auntie with her polythene boot stuck in a ventilator.

The clothing people take a regular belting as well. They have to watch a day-long succession of heads, bursting up through their Scandinavian sweaters like feeding-time in the ostrich house. They can still smile bravely at a mountainous matron in leather, scowling from the depths of a PVC hood and tell her she looks fine when, in fact, she looks like an old Sherpa porter who'd lost his expedition.

Then there's the man with a grievance. You can pick him out as if he was wearing a barrel. He goes towards a stand at a half-trot with his head wagging and a thin anticipatory smile of scorn such as one uses prior to dissecting a christmas cracker in search of cap and gift. He looks as if his farthingale had crept with all that literature stuffed in his pockets and, as often as not, he has one of those prehensile upper lips wagging like something on the sole of your shoe. Some stand attendants clap on wig and beard and mingle with the crowd to examine their own exhibits.

The buyer, too, can be spotted. He'll have to buy something, if it's only a comic cork. He shuttles to and fro with his wallet throbbing and an expression of dour joylessness. You'll find him in dark corners fumbling with his brochures. You'll see him again, twenty yards from the hire-finance people, slapping his back hair down and trying to work his tremulous chops into a mask of stern reliability. When he signs, his shaky hand will draw a dotted line as if trying to tattoo it. I've seen a buyer scuttling back and forth between bank and boat like a mating woodcock in a trench coat.

We got moving again and went after clacks and the rest of the stuff. Harry had a medicine bottle that he wanted filled with colza oil. He bought a khaki helmet with fur flaps that gave him an indignant heraldic look like a gyrfalcon. He also bought a rubber flipper to nail over his exhaust, a pound of assorted toggles, ten washers, a wim-wom, a chrome towel rail that he insisted was a sheer pole, a glass fibre sink to cover his binnacle and a needle-sharp, anodized, styled speedboat mast.

'It just shows,' he said, '. . . and you said I wouldn't find a dolphin striker.'

—And I'll wipe

If there's one thing calculated to make the laughter die in your throat it is the sight of a stack of empty cocoa mugs by the first light of dawn. Like a lonely traveller passing the gibbet, we hasten on our way for'ard.

Volunteers for washing up are usually young tyros first-timing at sea and anxious to prove themselves good chaps.

'That lad shows willing!' they imagine the owner confiding to his mate. If they turned around smartly from their dank little grottos it would be to see owner, mate and crew slinking quietly up the companionway and rolling the foxy eye of artifice.

Your Class III offshore racer, where the man with the dry bongrace is highly suspect and a salt-caked smoke-stack is the order of the day, leaves little room for the womanly arts. With your cook bounding up and down on his stool as if he were learning to bump saddle on a Sunday morning half-dollar trot, washing up is limited to a few cabalistic passes with the mop and the flicked forefinger for the obstinate bean. A skilled cook can rattle the helmsman's busk two shots out of three.

The most idyllic of galley layouts isn't proof against a smart turn to windward. Crammed with the grisly relics of a meal enjoyed east of Hurst, the sink lurks waiting for the duty men. Their little cries of revulsion wring all but the stoutest hearts, and luckier men avert their eyes as if they'd happened upon a beach-changer spiritedly trying to thrust both feet into one leg of his trousers. The paper towel and the cardboard plate pose a new threat. We come upon grave men sighting along their crockery under the cook's malignant gaze, and in American anchorages the air is filled with the hum of skimming plates as soon as the sun goes down. Many a guest breathing brandy and lifting his feet as if he were negotiating a flower-bed has sent his cap skimming out over the water and raised his cardboard soup-plate with old-world gallantry as he took his leave.

Apart from the exhibitionists who chance their luck at making scrambled egg, breakfast wash-ups are simple affairs. The cereal men, silently studying the packet instructions for becoming A Friend of Yogi Bear, offer no problems and paper tissues impart a gloss finish to greasy plates. Lunch – tomato soup in mugs and cold beef (after cautious sniffing) – leaves no legacy of hate either, but the evening meal is a ceremony that may mark a man. I have seen stoves festooned with calcified custard that would turn the edge of a chipping hammer, grill-pans welded to the cabin sole with leathern thongs of Welsh rarebit, and interesting little cameos in curry which couldn't be bettered by an exploding tinned pudding.

Volunteer cooks, who usually shamble home from work and wait like baby owls to be spoon fed, suddenly embark upon vast and pretentious meals that involve every pan in the ship save one – exempted because of its size, shape and

13

pedals. Poring over the instructions on the tin like professors with a baffling hunk of Dead Sea Scroll, they heft tin after tin of stewed steak into the spreading bog of garden-fresh tinned peas, and then plaster the galley with it like free-style artists working with busbys. The lot of the washer-up is a grim one. The cook, assuming that air of nobility proper to one who has grown frail in the service of others, drags himself on deck to the congratulatory cheers of the diners. The little group at the sink mutters its thanks through compressed lips.

For those who wash up in plastic bowls, tea-spoons are the greatest worry. Search how you may for the last spoon in the bowl it always goes over the side with the slops. Even when ashore yachtsmen ration them grudgingly at table. I have seen sailing hostesses at Mayoral functions who would leap forward and snatch the spoon from his Worship's saucer with a harsh cry of 'AHH, only one spoon for stirring!' The plastic bowl still has the edge on yacht sinks with central plugs which will only drain as the ship goes through stays. The sight of a lonely figure waiting like a terrier at a rat-hole, ready to thumb the slops down the spout as the ship slices in towards Portland Bill, is harsh stuff for the sentimentalist.

Old Harry, last rampart of a more graceful age, sees no problem in washing up. At table and with his frying pan handle vibrating under the brisk tattoo of his knife and fork (turned inboard out of deference for the diner seated opposite), one may see him finish his simple meal by buffing it with his bread until it would make the Mount Palomar telescope look like the dog's bowl. Not that he cannot produce a tea-towel (size eighteen collar) when required. With his engine running to provide a ready supply of hot rust, he has the laugh of scorn for those who question his domestic skills. He lacks a hand on the tiller on these occasions, and fellow yachtsmen have learned to recognize the significance of a boiling bow-wave and the massive melton rump visible over the side, and make proper adjustment to course and speed in good time.

All in favour

Annual general meetings, unless preceding a sausage supper or some other Bacchanalian revel, tend to be as well attended as a basketry class on a wet Monday night. The re-election of club officers should be a time of quiet joy with everybody trying to pretend that having the same bunch back in the saddle again is a personal triumph.

'Oh I see he's managed to get in then,' is no way to acclaim a new Commodore either. It hints at an undignified scuffle at the door and men swiping wildly with their caps at a fleet-footed candidate.

The Drill Hall, where the Chairman and his cullies sit on a low stage under a misleading fringe of cardboard palm trees, is no setting for an AGM. Two hours on a tubular chair, and the keenest member has polished his worsted to a racing finish by the uneasy orbiting of his aching acreage. No wonder it's hard to find a quorum.

'I haven't got a quorum,' pleads the Hon Sec pitifully, peering under tables.

Extraordinary general meetings called to consider the threat of a municipal sanitary Taj Mahal to the dinghy park, or the AGM's of National Associations are another matter. What feasts of oratory! What a show of hands – a grisly sight at fitting-out time. Not even the defeated speakers are cast down. They continue their harangue to their neighbours who stare fixedly ahead and murmur tactful agreement as if planting a drunk on a bus.

A well-attended AGM is a rewarding experience. The presentation of annual accounts is proposed and seconded with uncanny speed, while tweedy members from the sticks are still lurching to their feet and framing a searching question. The election of Flag Officers with their carefully compounded lovable-old-Joe expressions, hinting at rock-like integrity and resolve, goes with a swing (despite the vote which includes the limp and reluctant hands of members who lack the moral courage to fold their arms and sweat it out). Not until we come to 'Any other business' does the real treat begin though.

A fully paid-up member has invented a yardstick and doesn't know what to do with it; a retired major from Peebles who is a man of scientific bent and has sawn more catamarans down the middle than Forte has served hot-dogs, wants a ruling on fully battened trousers for trapeze crews; there is the matter of whether a cream tea and a doss in the attic is adequate recompense for a lecturing Trinity House Elder.

The man who is about to speak can be singled out. He gradually extends the neck while rocking to and fro on his buttocks and glaring at the Chair with his eyebrows topped up.

There is always a little man with a tuning-pipe voice who has sat out the meeting in mounting tension, awaiting 'any-other-business' time. He is a delegate. He makes three abortive attempts to rise, frustrated each time by more athletic director-material type speakers. At last, encouraged by a nod from the Chair, he makes it, half-crouching as if feeling the lack of belt and braces. His long-rehearsed bombshell has the impact of a wet newspaper parcel. The Chairman leans forward with kindly incredulous smile and cups his hand to his ear as if making the best of a flat battery.

Old Harry, happy where shot and shell fly thickest, never misses an AGM and is regularly thrown out of those belonging to other clubs. His flag officers note his arrival with sinking spirits, and front row do-it-yourself Disraelis resign themselves to a short and wobbly flight on wings of eloquence before being plucked and trussed by Harry's wet and windy rhetoric.

Rising slowly to convey an impression of utter weariness, his brooding gaze ranges the room and then, emphasizing each point with a stunning blow on the dome of the man in front, he launches into his peroration. Wherever men gather and talk his address on cocked hats for Commodores will be remembered with quiet admiration. Spellbound, the members listen, murmuring their approbation and gradually tiptoeing out of the room impatient to discuss his message.

The caretaker, respectfully sweeping around his boots and applauding under his breath, ducks a flailing fist, throws the main switch and leaves the key in the door.

A nice cup of tea

A lethal and lukewarm half-inch of tannin

No package tourist abroad, poking around in his bouillabaisse with wary concentration as if clearing a stopcock, can view the dish with more distrust than your Briton faced with the foreign teabag. Waving aside the proffered lemon with furrowed brow, he prods and presses the contents of his teapot in the vain hope of winning some vestige of flavour from that false brew. The gipsy fiddler,

17

contorting himself as if trying to get a number two jib out of a chain locker, sobs himself offstage unheeded.

There is a stalwart British belief that, provided you arm yourself with tea, you can wake a man at 0200 hours of a wet morning and expect to be thanked for it. He will sit bolt upright with a marble stare, while his wandering ghost returns to its earthly envelope with the reluctance of a railway booking clerk turning to his window. In any case brewing up under way is uncannily productive of trouble. Alerted by the whistling kettle our owner at once begins peering around keenly. 'Ready about,' he roars, timing it to perfection. A cloud of steam and a harsh cry from below signal his success. 'Get that stuff out of the way until later,' he says in a voice rich with scorn, racing from wheel to chart and back.

The teabag has proved a great disappointment to Old Harry. His first experience, when he used (in error) an Insolvic Bilge Pak, produced a unique brew which he has since sought in vain. He was able to dispense with shaving for six weeks and his breath was fatal to death-watch at twenty paces. At fitting out time in the yacht yard the flipped teabag finds some curious billets. The week-end public in carcoat and Cossack cap stops a barrage from all sides. 'It's worth keeping your eye open,' notes a bargain hunter unwisely; a naturalist mistakenly noting the flight of the pipistrelle bat, ' 'gainst darking sky at eventide', stops one slap in his specimen box.

Old Harry, who learnt his art at the knee of a trawler cook, will brew up off Dover, top up off the Nab and thereafter add water, tea and molasses at each change of watch until his crew is sucking in his cheeks like an autoclave. The expressions 'Let me give you a fresh cup', and 'How many spoons?' take on a new and grim significance. Old Harry's tea will riddle an enamel mug so that it can be played like a bassoon, and any teaspoon ungalvanized will look like part of the Sutton Hoo ship-find inside a fortnight.

Early morning tea in the average hotel is a battle of wills. You approach the desk where a woman wearing a black firehose sneers at the cut of your suit, 'I'd like tea for two at seven,' you pipe. She sighs and passes you over to the porter who writes it down. You get tea for seven at 0200, no milk and somebody else's shoes.

The club tea-urn, traditional scene of wifely rivalry, is also the centre of dinghy sailing acrimony. Lay-about social members with knitting bags knock off the cup-cakes and reduce the contents of the urn to a lethal and lukewarm half-inch of tannin just as the first of the Hornet boys, shedding water like a crop-sprayer, staggers through the door. Old Harry, who will flash up that urn until it is rocking and jetting steam like a carousel, has been forcibly restrained since the occasion of the Grand Opening of the Mulch Bottom Sailing Club drying room which the Lady Mayor, corseted like Norman knight, graciously consented to perform.

A small girl, all knee-sock and frilly knicker, came forward with a floral spray, but her Worship, stepping on a duckboard, projected a lustier spray via a knothole straight up her Regalia, soaking her civic pride. Her sharp bark of alarm reduced the child to howls and cued the town band into a spirited rendering of Rule Britannia. Old Harry, sizing up this critical impasse, hauled off a mug of his best, removed the matchstick from the hole in his tin of condensed, and blew a milky jet which, gaining in pressure what it lacked in accuracy, wandered selectively up and down the Commodore's features. Her Worship, sampling the brew, drew a long and shuddering breath which she did not exhale until some minutes later, when she rose from her rostrum to tug the cord and unveil the boiler, revealing Old Harry's combination suit, staked out to dry like the pelt of some mythical beast.

Any Questions

– an easy nonchalant air

There was never the lecturer born whose heart didn't throb with pride as he braced himself for the applause. From personal experience it sounds like six wet teabags pattering on a tin tray.

Preparation is the thing, we're told, and *know* your subject inside out. Winter is the lecture season, and autumn finds the shaving-mirror comics already rehearsing their stuff. Take any crowded train and whip away that barrage of newspapers and what will you find? A row of faces mouthing and grimacing like drama school, and enough notes between the lot of them to jam a hay-baler.

Notes made on slips of cardboard are risky.

It gets on men's minds. I've seen ticket collectors with the peaks of their caps vibrating with concentration as they studied a slip of pasteboard headed: 'With Phoebe to Finland – A Troublesome Night'. I've also seen men on their hind legs, lips as dry as Peter Pan's whistle, faced by fifty rustling club members, and gagging over a season ticket.

On THE NIGHT you adopt an easy, nonchalant air. You steal an occasional fascinated glance at the rows of chairs and the scaffold itself. Then you are being led to the stage . . .

You try a smile, but it emulsifies into a sort of aristocratic sneer – like a stiff-necked and arrogant Don Pedro surveying his peons from the hacienda.

You should try to grip your audience from the onset. I have seen audiences gripped by their onsets and they never recovered. You should win their interest. I once won it and held it the whole way through, only to find I had a game chip stuck to my dewlap.

Having been announced by the Chairman, who says how lucky everyone is to have you there and hints at the goodies in store, you lumber slowly to your feet and give them your loon's smile. It feels like an elastic band over your mouth. You shuffle. The one-handed claps die down. Everybody settles back. They look at you with the wary, unconvinced scrutiny of a dog faced with a plastic bone.

'Mister Coddomore, Officers . . .'

A chemical change takes place. Your coat collar rides up and your sleeves recede. Your palms turn to defrosted fillets, your stomach feels like a turnip in a string bag and your hands swell. They become unmanageable. One tries to crawl into your pocket, the other nips on to the table and sits there like a great red toad. The audience embarks upon an orgy of shuffling, coughing, hitching of chairs and match-striking.

What you need is a gimmick. A shirt front that lights up

and flashes every five . . . a stick insect behind your ear. The rest is easy.

Nowadays we rarely see the good old-fashioned, water-sipping lecturer who rumbles away behind a blackboard. Instead, endless picture shows at odd angles, commented on by a disembodied tweet from a pool of shadow.

'. . . And here we are again in the canal . . .' intones a voice. '. . . there's a good shot of mother on a bollard.' They start every sentence with 'Here we are' or 'Then we went'. Take away their films and there they stand mumbling their monosyllables and rolling their eyes like a hammed-up scene from *Uncle Tom's Cabin*.

After-dinner speeches are no easier. Nowadays every speaker concentrates on being a comic. I visualized a time when every guest speaker will come bounding on, holding up long, baggy trousers and firing off starting pistols, yelling: 'Ello, 'ello, 'ello, 'ere we are again, oh dear, oh dear, oh dear.'

You must have one funny story, and say that 'it reminds you of the time when . . .'

Timing matters, too. It's possible to rehearse a lecture mentally and take two solid interest-packed hours over it, and then get up on the stage and babble the lot all inside twenty minutes and be left with a question-time that dies on you. 'Any more?' you implore, smiling like Joey. An uneasy audience gazes back, exuding pity and racking brains. Somebody asks an oblique question about pooping.

'Ah, I'm glad you asked that', you lie. However, pooping is good for half an hour of anybody's time. You drone on.

You must avoid ending up with anti-climax – like an indoor firework to top off a Guy Fawkes display. That apologetic beseeching glance you shoot at the nodding Chairman has a lot of similarity to the last despairing little puff of green smoke which is the grand finale of some cardboard Vesuvius.

The Chairman wakes with a grunt and smacks his lips. He says how sorry those members were who were unlucky enough to have to leave to catch buses. He thanks you and leads the applause. You could make more row with a pastry brush.

You travel home uneasily, surprised at the sudden popularity of bus-riding.

Find me a shakedown

When I was a lad (a six foot cadaver in father's trousers, all ears and knee-caps), open meetings were as rare as trouser-clips in the Ascot enclosure. These days the dinghy boys spend their time belting from one open meeting to the next with a flat wallet and a healthy smile. The little man in the wet woollen hat, dragging a muddy canvas bag filled

23

with crumpled shirts is a familiar figure to seaside landladies. It's getting so that the sharp intakes of breath along Marine Crescent, as the week-end regiment of dinghy sailors slap wetly up to the front doors, sounds like a panel of judges at a Miss Bikini contest. A landlady in fair training can spot a bobble-cap at two miles. You'd stand more chance carrying a cello.

It's becoming a major problem for club secretaries.

'Oh, we can always find you a bed,' they say, rooting around in the hedge bottom. 'We can always fix you up with a shakedown.'

I've been shaken down so thoroughly that dawn has found me grunting and groaning to an accompanying arpeggio of whanging springs on cast iron beds that looked like models of the Forth Bridge. I've shuffled around the room on air beds that expired at 3.00 a.m. and left me searching for bungs by match-light.

I've racketed around on a put-me-up with a cuckoo clock and a scratching dog for company, and spent nights on canvas beds that spat the pillows off the end at ten minute intervals and creaked like a ship in a gale. Nor must we forget our old friend 'the make-shift on the landing' where somebody's father, late home and breathing hard, begins to feel thoughtfully along your jowls in the dark.

That of course is what is known as 'accommodation in members' homes'! It goes with a two-chime bell and a porch light that makes you look like the Quatermass Experiment. Your hostess smiles like a split sack, and boots her Iron Jelloids out of sight under the sofa. It also goes with no bolt to the bathroom door.

This is a sign of family healthy-mindedness and you're supposed to yell out cheerily 'I'm in' when anyone tries the door. This arrangement has you shuffling to and fro between door and plumbing in a nightmare Cossack dance. The bathroom is the fulcrum of family life – try getting in before your host and you shatter his routine.

'*He's* in there,' they hiss.

Wait until last and there'll be a row of accusing faces

waiting breakfast for you. You'll take to listening at the door before you try the handle, and your hostess, looking like a Grenadier Guards RSM in chiffon, will whip open the door and catch you pretending to examine the bannister.

You may prefer to be independent and try your luck in lodgings. A couple of nights in one of those towering narrow 'guest houses,' haunted by the rank ghosts of a thousand plates of limp cabbage and laminated meat loaf, is enough to take the wicker out of a man. A bedroom with a hospital trolley in a chintz kilt and a rocking tallboy full of clangorous hangers that chime and racket like a hand-bell semi-final as you fumble for the door in the dark. Three flights of stairs to a bathroom on the landing which has a WC that bellows its message to the sleeping household no matter how gently you play it – and a huge iron bath with claws that clutch iron knobs as if at any moment it would hurl a volley at you.

Try asking for a front door key during breakfast. Rows of old ladies with white hair and pink scalps all guarding their private packets of cereals will glance up covertly looking for signs of dissipation. After a night in a bed shaped like the Bowl of Death they are not disappointed.

The traditional landlady has almost disappeared. The old black spider with the bog oak brooch has given way to the hostess in a flowering house-coat and a wagging cigarette who '*loves* people'.

Some boroughs actually encourage us, but a corporation barbecue in a flogging tent on the rain-swept beach – sausages on sticks and flat beer in paper cups – followed by a five minutes harangue by the Mayor who quotes 'Messing about in boats' as he edges towards the door, is hardly my idea of making the welkin ring.

Stag at bay

It's around this time of year that the antlers on the hall-stand come in for their annual punishment. Our revellers returning from Men's Supper Night at the club can never resist that mirth-provoking pantomime of crashing around the sitting-room wearing those dusty relics and chanting, 'Look dear, I've been to a shtag party.' Mother, wearing housecoat and skin food, watches from the doorway with the grim detachment of a theatre critic at a mummer's play.

Since women first invaded our clubs and the tide of cress sandwiches rolled in, unchecked, to envelop the bar, this annual demonstration of male independence and defiant self-assertion has become a stern necessity. Yachtsmen have been driven into smaller and smaller smoke rooms until, straight-lipped, but unbowed, they make their last British square around the gas meter under the stairs. From a cane chair in the annexe, the ladies have advanced in tight whist drive formation.

Where once the eyeballs rolled through that acrid fog of cigar smoke, we now have Doris slapping butter on scones as if she were building a wall. Gone is the rumble of male conversation and the art of the brandy raconteur. In its place are those steaming matriarchs of the tea-urn – Brenda, looking like a bumblebee in her brushed wool sweater, and Cynthia of the stale cheese fingers (who starves her husband). Give credit where it's due, the golden goddess in the candy-striped shorts is a good kid and a fine little helmswoman, but let her keep her griddle cakes away from the bread-and-butter brigade or it'll be, 'Sheila darling, you look *frozen* in that bikini, positively *grey*.'

With the approach of Men's Supper Night 'they' hope that we won't make disgusting spectacles of ourselves again. We allow ourselves a tolerant chuckle. It is always we who see the rest of the boys home, not *our* heels that plough twin furrows across the kitchen lino. We will be the survivors who stand in swaying conclave at the club door, nodding gravely at each other and contemplating Percy on the launching trolley.

The 'supper', which is a symbolic touching of food, gets into its stride with the disposal of the speechmakers. The absent ladies, filling their own coal scuttles, pause to listen to the distant, eerie howling borne on the frosty night air and permit themselves a cracked chuckle. The Commodore, treading carefully and smiling like a split orange, takes his departure while his tie remains unshorn.

It is a night of traditional song and story. Nose to magnificent nose, our mariners bawl the adventures of Anthony Roly while the Vice Commodore, who stayed on, sobs out his heart at the sheer majesty of the harmony. Elsewhere the mood may take scientific turn, and exponents of racing law ('sheeriously ol' man) ply their art with game chip and salt cellar. Old Harry, frowning at the heaving deck beneath his stockinged feet, departs to tap the bar clock, watching the falling minute hand with growing alarm.

There will be a strange lack of recollection about the journey home. Perhaps a vague memory of Old Harry, a figure of military dignity in paper hat and cropped tie, sitting in a bus shelter waiting for it to start, and another lonely figure arguing about the five-minute rule with a snow-capped pillar box, otherwise only a dim succession of lamp posts and shadowy guilt concerning no-parking signs.

At the garden gate we will halt out of consideration for the neighbours while we finish the last stanza of *Over the hill brother*, before applying our several latch-keys to the coal-house door while Percy lines up the milk bottles again. It is such scenes as this – little cameos of brother unity – which give us our stature in the eyes of our women.

Let us then drink a toast to the many absent friends who

went out to look at the weather and couldn't find it. Let us drink also to that man of indomitable courage, Old Harry, who 'made a fine exhibition of himself', and retained his male dignity right up to that moment when, quivering with indignation, he stormed into the wardrobe, slammed the door shut and demanded the ground floor.

Come and join us

Sooner or later you'll be invited for the week-end – advice for the starry-eyed.

If Gentle Reader ranks as a novice (a term which always smacks of hay-seeds and a flat check cap) he'd better be on

his guard, for sooner or later he'll be invited for a 'little week-end' afloat. I've seen week-end guests stagger ashore to seize a handful of the good earth and kneel there cackling with maniacal glee to see it trickle through their fingers.

The guests will find father, mother, 'our big boy', and a silent man in a competent cap and short boots as his fellow rovers. The cruise will start with 'an easy day's sail' across the bay. In actual fact, it'll be a wild bang to windward with everyone leaping around like a comic paper-hanging act.

Our tyro will be put on a winch, 'No old man, the other way round,' and then taken off it after building up more riding turns than a gymkhana and losing the handle. He may even have a suspected fractured wrist. Whichever happens he'll sit in a corner of the cockpit wearing that monstrous new yachting cap bought for the occasion, and try to look keenly alert to what's going on.

Later there will be tomato soup in mugs. This will contrast nicely with his green face. With that crimson ringed mouth under the canopy of white plastic and patent leather, he'll look like a cross between a werewolf and a novelty pepper pot. His ravaged features will twist into a shaky smirk of rapture at the offer of a second mug, refusing it only on the grounds of repletion. Shortly after that he'll have changed to an inanimate hump on the lee coaming, and everyone will become distantly sympathetic and exchange meaningful glances.

Finding an 'anchorage' is the next adventure. It will leave an atmosphere of hostility aboard for some time afterwards and won't be referred to again until father sees fit to make laughing reference to it. In they sail, father on tiptoes and everybody else crouching at his feet holding fenders. The scene is reminiscent of St Francis preaching to the birds.

Every yacht in the anchorage will be on the alert, as father comes swerving in under sail. Every crew is on deck wishing him well ('Good grief, what's the fool trying to do?') and his passage will be studied by a tense audience like medical students watching a dissection. Our guest has been made to stand in the companionway, the very personification of redundancy, and his one attempt to peer up out of his lair is met with a shrill chorus of 'Get your head down!' He sinks from view like a cinema organist playing himself off.

After the first splash of anchor and rattle of chain, there will be the 'move under power' – the normal sequence to finding an anchorage under sail. This is undertaken as soon as mother comes on deck with the tea, and is really the result of a lost battle of nerves between father, who anchored exactly where he meant to, and a tall man on the boat in line astern who stands silently on his bows calculating the distance of father's stern. He finally goes down on one knee and reads the name on the offending stern and notes it in a little book. The loss of the first and last letters lends a disturbingly foreign flavour which even father with his defaced ensign is hard put to dispel.

A 'good wholesome meal' comes next. Mother sends up a blast of oily smoke and flame from her paraffin stove and calls for volunteers to peel spuds. Our guest, who has given a day-long exhibition of imbecility, nausea and monumental obstructionism, comes to life and begins larding on a demonstration of conscience-goaded servility like the dog that pinched the chops.

Father, who saw the bucket of spuds, hastily spreads a chart out and studies it with blank concentration, his taut rump stuck out in the companionway. At supper everybody is full of health and good fellowship and our guest, still uncomfortably aware of covert inspection, goes so far as to show 'our big boy' a trick with matches but burns a hole in a table mat. He just catches father rolling his eyes to heaven – hastily disguised as a sudden interest in the skylight.

The 'good night's rest' is a natural follow-on. The guests may be in the forepeak, along with the Baby Blake, snug in a flea-bag which is a foot too short and makes him look like a huge flannelette moth in the act of emerging from its chrysalis.

Then follows a night of unforgettable eventfulness. It will begin with 'dragging the anchor', a game to be played by both young and old, and continues with 'dinghy under the counter', winding up at dawn with a visit from the Harbour Master who says, 'You're in the fairway.' The whole night will be a vague nightmare of pyjama-clad figures shuddering over a muddy winch, a howling engine, voices, lights, mother in a quilted wrap looking like a Chinese peasant straight from *The Good Earth* trying to dispense tea, and father oddly inarticulate, tip of lower jaw unaccountably meeting tip of nose, mumbling 'Framfiff' and (to 'our big boy'), 'Go and feff my field glaffefs!'

There's no waking up from this nightmare – there's still the 'hearty breakfast' and the 'fine run home' to be enjoyed, and – who knows? – the guest may be allowed to try his hand at the wheel!

It's the thought that counts

– not the contents of the parcel

The man who can tear off the Christmas wrapping of his present and sob out his delighted gratitude for scavenge pump, sack of calibrated stud-link or Insolvic Bilge Pack is

lucky. There is more Hey-ho-the-holly in a much needed strum box than in any bucket of assorted nautical cuff-links or mermaid-embossed piece of neck-wear ('Why it's a tie!'), which looks regrettably like the Ocean Racing gribble at ten paces.

The little woman went off novelty ear-rings the time she shook her head and lobbed a shackle pin and a couple of art jubilee clips into the Commodore's cream of chicken – she ceased to split her sides at comic tea-towels years ago. Impressive matrons, with a vast frontage of high rateable value and a hairdo like a fibreglass busby, lack only the jackstaff and a couple of Oerlikons when they are wearing their sidelights.

The head-scarf question has just about reached maximum impact too. I have seen a maiden with the English Channel Middle Sheet printed across the top of her dome, come out of the RYA cocktail party with fixes firmly plotted from frontal to occipital, and a couple of navigators in hot pursuit anxious to show how they cheated the tide off Les Hanois. It's much the same with those gay skirts, covered in reproductions of the yacht designer's laughable art – a girl has to have a smart turn of speed if she is to thwart Old Harry, and his determination to study her table of offsets.

It is never very easy to discover just what that venerable seafarer wants for Christmas, since he is rarely to be found. The series of deafening explosions which herald the dark evenings and his experiments with his carbide bicycle lamp, coincide with a course of nocturnal expeditions to the saltings adjoining the timber wharf. Now and then, maybe, the stray beam from a car headlight may pick out a little tableau of frozen mobility, revealing a cross-cut saw thrust hastily under a bush, and an attempt to juggle weathered features into a vacuous mask of good citizenship. Otherwise his movements pass unnoticed.

You can't go wrong giving him another knife of course. Old Harry has enough knives stacked away to stock a trading post, but he still sticks to a ten inch rip-hook honed to a parrot's beak and thrusting lethally out of its sheath. I have seen him turn smartly and bring down a topsail and three pairs of trousers with that scythe.

Knife-buying should be left to men, though. A woman will fall for a hoop-iron cake-knife in tooled leather holster with Minnihaha bead fringe, or one of those compendiums which include every device from a scalpel to a dottle-scraper. Men – who realize that there is no edge as keen as a touch of desperation and a shirt tail in the sheet winch, tend to fall for the modern trend in buttock-hung workshop, complete with knife, spike, shifting spanner and anvil. As long as the foredeck hand looks as if he is about to tile a roof, he is properly equipped.

Outside the circle of hearth and home, present-buying is conducted along realistic lines based upon 'she-didn't-put-herself-out-much-last-year' principles. We see anxious harbingers of Christmas joy scavenging the economy novelty counter as if they were riddling coal.

'It's the thought that matters,' they laugh uneasily, wrapping up their sixth joke key-ring in holly-berry paper. They never see the effect of these tokens of friendship upon their recipients. Like that grave inquiry of 'Would you like to see the cheeseboard, sir?' they evoke the lifted lip of disgust, and do about as much to make the wild bells ring out as the paper decorations in a branch-line waiting room.

Old Harry, who either makes his own presents, or shops with disturbing originality at the Railway Lost Property Office, is a figure to be feared by Post Office clerks at Yuletide. In festive mood he advances with his marline-lashed hummocks of good cheer, and then roars his protest as the scales blur with the speed of revolution and hit zero with a clang like a moneylender's till. Officials rally to point out the snares attached to packing cans of home-brewed ship-worm inhibitor, and to agree that, while attractive place mats can be made from old coir hawser (flipping sandhoppers out of the Health Insurance stamps), they weigh less if dried beforehand.

There is plenty of scope though. Code flag jewellery is always acceptable, and the useful gift finds a grateful friend.

Mabel in her little angora wrap with England Expects ... coded across her sternum, would bring a lump to any throat, and old dad with his braces checked away to hide his occulting nylon American-style socks, appreciates a gift of distinction.

It's a wild duck table-mat to a plastic gull on an ashtray that we will get the usual stack of cards, featuring voluminous galleons peppered with bird-shot from our in-laws, and if jolly Uncle Ned doesn't send us the annual comic cork it will be because we failed to send him his annual comic bottle-opener last year.

The long trot

During Cowes Week the trots sometimes seem to be a Sargasso absorbing all boats – the life of the denizens is as open to the onlooker as the shops of an Eastern bazaar

Whenever we attend Cowes Week and moor in the trots we hang more motor tyres round us than medals of merit on a baker's diploma. We need them. I've seen a tubby little cruiser go into that Sargasso of squawking fenders and

get spat out a week later rating as a Thirty Square. It's like a garden party with everyone trying to get near the celebrity without being caught actually shoving – very polite, but watch your footwork if you don't want a flattened hacking-flap.

You moor fore and aft between buoys, then in comes another boat and hangs on to you. It goes on like that until the last arrivals can step ashore dry-shod. There are the non-cricketing creeps who don't even take their lines to the buoys and you get under way with two a side and one of them towing stern-first. We once got as far as Calshot when a man in spotted pyjamas came on deck and went to the rail. Then he panicked. He had delicate reasons for being on the wrong boat, and we fixed him up with a false beard and he caught the ferry back to Cowes mingling with a ladies' bowls team.

We've laid alongside another boat which also had motor tyre fenders (no treads), and every time the tide turned we had to change gear. The owner was one of these 'live the good life' boys with his back hair hanging down his transom and a sack of turnips on his foredeck. He had his bowsprit stuck through somebody's porthole, and there was an ancient yachtsman peering closely at it thinking it was some sort of memorial plaque.

With all that mass of boats around there's never a dull moment. You can watch Fastnet veterans mirthlessly weighing each other's trousers before a race, cruising cat owners explaining the proper way out to short-sighted oarsmen, short men in long shorts fiddling with their burgees and stout men in gay play suits trying not to look like 'Bo Bo' at a Chimp's Tea Party. At night you'll hear the plaintive calls of lost guests trying to find their ships. Cries of 'Where are you Butter-Cup?' (pronounced 'Batter-Cap') bring every plastic-topped Rear-Commodore in the fleet foaming on deck.

Then there is always an old Eight Metre with a concrete keel, converted to a cut-down cruiser so slow in stays that, beating down harbour, she gets engulfed. There'll be a string

35

of droopy washing, a fierce-eyed, shaggy young man, a cat, a baby in a hoodless pram and a girl in a dirndl skirt. Everybody will be wonderfully kind about it. The trouble is that their paint will come off on other people's fenders, which will come off on other people's topsides, etc. Sometime during the Week this family will accidentally set light to a sack.

The boatwork is worth watching. Try persuading a healthy British family to climb on the tea-wagon and they'll exchange level glances and point their nostrils at you, but on the trots you'll see father wearing a nodding woollen Knickerbocker Glory, rowing a tiny pram stacked with relations all with their huge knees drawn up like pole-squatting fakirs and gazing around with unabashed serenity. Then there's the 'Look-I-can-scull' yachtsman standing up and wagging away with a look of pained concentration until he hits a taut warp. You see them strung out and kicking on these warps like *kebabs* on a spit.

If you don't want to trust your dinghy to the half-dozen assorted Adam Faiths at the landing steps, who mind boats by plying for hire in them, you can always snuggle down on board and listen in at a good ventilator, but for real entertainment you watch for late arrivals trying to find a berth.

In they come down-wind, down-tide, travelling like the Edinburgh express, making for any boat whose owner hasn't been quick enough to whip someone else's dinghy alongside and switch his gaze abstractedly in another direction. They approach with eyes starting from sockets, knuckles gleaming white, hair on end like a busby and crew galloping round with fenders like ants waving eggs.

'May I come alongside, Sir?' they plead pitifully as they go past clutching their way out of sight through a gap in the ranks ahead. They have that same air of urgent departure that old Harry had the time he went searching for the cloakroom and reappeared on stage among the potted palms.

There is a noticeable reluctance for yachtsmen to raise their voices above conversation level no matter how urgent the situation, and it is considered a little theatrical to use the introductory 'Ahoy'. An owner is far happier clearing his throat and saying, 'I say there!' in a slightly stronger-than-life tone as he sweeps to destruction. It's a pity because when you're being carried beam-on down the trots clanging merrily from bow to bow, the man who can roar 'I . . . am . . . not . . . under . . . control' has it cap and pants over the knuckle-gnawer who stands ashen-faced and shrills orders and apologies, while his scalp feels taut as a new school cap and his heaving line falls in a sodden tangle three feet outboard.

At the same time each night you get the jolly revellers coming off searching for their ships. 'This isn't ours, Roger,' they roar, peeling back your protective flap of blanket. They come steeple-chasing over your decks – great downy-chinned youths with anklebones stuck out like signals and club ties down to their knees.

This steeple-chasing over decks is continuous. If you're moored on the inside you get the lot. 'May we cross?' they honk, flattening you into your mess of groats as you crouch at lunch.

There's a noticeable reluctance to cross those huge, high cruisers, though. There's something about that baleful battery of Crookes' lenses under strawberry blonde birds' nests, staring from articulated chairs that makes a man step through open hatches. You never know whether to labour up over the coach-roof or bumble through the sun-deck cocktail party, dragging your boiling fowl in its string bag behind you.

There's a daily exodus just before racing begins when British self-control can be seen at its apoplectic best. There'll be an enormous tarry lugger beam-on to a battened-down ocean racer, with her taut-lipped crew narrowing their eyes so much that they can't see which way is out, and a man in a linen hat who looks like one of the Flower Pot Men, trying to get an X-boat to jump over a festoon of warps. The undertone of well modulated bleating sounds like a sheep-dog trial in the distance.

Give me Firework night. I recall a yachtswoman dressed

entirely in canvas from head to foot who watched the whole breathtaking display without uttering any other words than ... 'Rahther lovely!' as each salvo hit the heavens. It was not my fault that Old Harry chose that night to forget to make a hole in the tinned pudding before boiling it. The roar of disintegrating suet just gave her time to get the first syllable out before the pan started on its way down.

Severing old ties

Those shattered bibs that cascade down our 'quick-knits' ...

Wearing a club tie wins us the lifted eyebrow of respect from casual passers-by.

'Aha', they say, 'a sailing man, eh?' – noting our clear eye and panther-like tread.

Permit me my *moue* of gentle protest. There are men wearing these emblems of the deep who have never known what it is to walk with the slack-knee'd shuffle of a man who is half an inch ahead of his wet trouser seat.

If there is one garment a man is reluctant to renew it's that ragged club rope-work around his neck. A new tie (we only buy the cheaper rayon models when nobody's watching) can cause a man to be mistaken for a new member, liable to be lumbered with a fresh stack of club loan debentures and prey for club bores who'll be after him with their mossy old yarns like starlings after wire-worm.

The 'better type' of yachtsman manages to wear his bodice

banner in a clean arch of perfection, revealing the motif-plainly. Not so with we red-wristed imposters who won our club membership on the strength of a corduroy cap and a trench coat with epaulettes. Try as we may, our anxious hours before the mirror produce only a shattered bib, binding the wings of our collars. Like the hastily lashed door to a bell tent, it cascades from view under a woolly labour-of-love in magenta quick-knit to spend its splendour across our navels.

Our shy and genuinely new member wears his stiff and vividly new neck-wear laid out across the front of his pullover like a mackerel on a slab, fearing that his right to admittance will be challenged unless it is in fair view. He takes up his position at the dark end of the bar between the salted nuts and the Lifeboat box, prepared to let go with a high, mad laugh whenever 'our' Commodore lets fall some little gem. Attention doesn't turn his way at first – then he notices the life-members watching him with shudders of revulsion and his gaze falls. He finds that his tie has sunk deep in his pint and is soaking up nutriment like a thirsty tapir.

The tie, which by accident or design, closely resembles that of another and nobler club, puts us in line for the old 'Belong to the Royal Cheesecutter Yacht Club, eh?' from some military fellow traveller with purple wattles. We explain about the Blatford Foundry Canteen SC. His smile slips down like a loose gum-shield.

'Really . . . I see,' he comments. The warmth of laughing good-fellowship goes out like six penn'th of hotel gas fire.

Old Harry, founder of the Gribble Creek Cruising Club, which has seven members, all on the committee, twelve annual dinners a year and old Harry as Treasurer and Commodore, invented his own tie and club regalia. The motif on the tie is tastefully executed in pink and mauve, and seems to represent crossed thigh boots on an old bicycle saddle. There was a time when his wife sent it to the dry cleaner, who returned it with a note of apology for failure to remove these 'stains'.

Let old Harry enter a strange club, and conversation dies to a rumble of concern as he recommends himself in the visitor's book and flips out his tie for approval. Nothing more is heard above the drumming of thumbs through the pages of Lloyd's.

His tie lives out most of its life on a nail in the bulkhead like a pathetic victim in a gamekeeper's 'larder', to be lifted down only when he goes ashore, and donned by dropping the bight over his cap as if lassoing a bollard. In his tubular trousers and self-made smock, and wearing this sad halter, he looks like one of the ten Good Men of Calais off to give himself up to the foe. The knot on that tie is drawn up tight to the size of a pea, and it is polished to the glaze of a doss-house bannister.

There are those of us who remember times when to wear your tie in a strange club was to go in fear of the scissor; many a fine trophy has been dragged forth into the light and revealed in all its custard-embossed glory before that devilish fate. Old Harry led many such a cutting-out expedition but pity won him over in the end. There was a night when he was weaving down the street at first light looking like a battered old gun-boat with bottled Bass thrusting in warlike batteries from every pocket. He turned the corner and came face-to-face with a clergyman's outing. The jig was up. His features twisted with pity. 'Poor devils . . .' he breathed. 'But dog-bite-me, what a party!'

Applied Seamanship

The art of being unspectacular

FOR MOST OF US, most of the time, it tends to be a bit spectacular. The approach to a marina berth with a following wind for instance; all we need for an act rich in healthy slapstick is the baggy check trousers, a Co-Co nose and an unlimited supply of flour, although anyone who has, like me, accidentally triggered off a dry powder fire extinguisher can dispense with the latter.

He hasn't got a clew

Until you've fisted a jib on a bowsprit end with your button holes spouting like a water cart you don't know what sail handling is like. Grandma fumbling with her chocolate digestives makes more row than the plastic crackle of a small modern cruiser in a blow. Your modern yachtsman could stuff one of those jibs in with his shirt tail and know no more until some lynx-eyed RORC man challenged his J measurement.

Not that a shift of wind on the five minute gun of a Southsea–Harwich race isn't good for some mirth. The excess crew hitherto banished below, their peaked and wistful faces straining at portholes for an unrewarding glimpse of alternate sea and sky, will be up on deck in a flash to shift the genoa. The careful owner will have a list of his sails on a bulkhead so that even a stranger to the ship can go at once to the correct bin. Percy, who is referred to as 'our new friend' and is present on the recommendation of his previous

owner (who refused to meet father's eye at the time), is dispatched at once to fetch the Number Two. Even as the ant will emerge from its hole to wave an egg idiotically before returning for another, so he shuttles back and forth with sail after sail.

'I would have thought it was a small thing to ask,' father confides to Class II and III.

Old Harry's mainsail, which has folds and wrinkles that would have stumped a Renaissance sculptor, is a direct challenge to the scientific mind; it casts a wind shadow like Wembley Stadium, and his apparent wind directs a blast skywards that you could juggle a beach ball on. The venturi effect, when he sets his jumbo jib, hits friend and foe alike with a jet of cutch-laden violence. I've seen trapeze riding dinghy boys shuttling up and down their masts like sash weights, and Class III navigators shaking their Ventimeters with impotent fury, I've known the time when he could slam about off Cowes and blast the struts off every deckchair on the Squadron lawn.

The yacht that ships Harry as a sail-handler reaps its own reward. Refusing to accept that a sail must not be fought at all times, he will fall upon it with his abdomen in the lightest of weather and, roaring encouragement to the owner who is underneath, he will fist it into a tight wad and stamp it down the forehatch. Mother in the galley making drop-scones applauds his skill as he withdraws his batter-spattered seaboot. At stopping up sails he has no master either. Vast pods of canvas sway aloft stopped with yarns specially rotted for the purpose in his hanging closet. A sharp command, a tug and the twang of a breaking halliard as that massive bundle, like some nightmare pupae, descends with stunning force just as mother emerges with the second batch of drop-scones.

On his own ship, light airs are viewed with sinking spirits by his guests. Radiating an atmosphere of gala and like one nursing a surprise treat, he orders the 'fancy kites' dragged on deck. With the ship shrouded in sagging expanses of mouldering duck as though awaiting the arrival of decorators, and smiling indulgently, he orders the boat away so that his crew may feast their eyes upon this singular sight.

It is no job for a fool to set the modern headsail of course. Backs to the pulpit, gaping trousers swallowing the cooling draughts of salt water, your modern foredeck jockey must pit his skill with the hanks against the man who is twitching the halliard, and the slob with the lean-to forehead back aft who is cranking the sheet winch before the sail is half out of its bag. For kicks though 'finding the clew' takes some beating. Like one of those playing-card spelling games (fun for young and old), it brings out the vicious streak. Give any healthy man a bag with a clew in it somewhere, plus a stopwatch and a leeward mark, and Percy is in for a brisketing.

Another favourite old refrain is,

'Oh-don't-let-Percy-bag-the-spinnaker', preferably accompanied on the nose-flute.

Hunched over a mound of hysterically coloured nylon looking for clews and pawing it over like a matron at the remnant counter, your man bagging his first spinnaker will live a haunted life until it is set. You can study their dream-poisoned sleep as their hands, restlessly searching for clews, tug experimentally at the ear which protrudes from the navigator's sleeping bag.

Setting the sail is the crowning achievement.

'Whenever you're ready,' calls the owner in his special little-boy-lost voice, following up with an introductory scream.

The sail billows out of its bag, takes station twenty yards to leeward at half mast height, and commences its un-dulatory flight. Percy soars up the mast on the halliard and jerks up and down like a hard collar on an anxious throat, determined to win fame if not glory by hanging on. A friendly hand grasps his trousers while he bicycles out of them into a seafaring future – on some other ship.

On the level

Drying out against the quay wall makes you feel conspicuous. It makes you feel uneasy too – sort of brooding, like a pavement artist out of chalk and watching a rain-cloud. There's another thing – you gather more experts around you than a trade luncheon, and all you can do about it is sit dangling your plumb-bob while the tide goes down.

You'll see a yachts-man sitting on his

sidedeck with the anchor in his lap, gnawing his knuckles in a fever of apprehension while he waits for his keel to settle. All you have to do is to creep up and twang his warps to see him go soaring up the rigging howling for his underwriter.

It's all a matter of seeing she lists in against the quay so she won't topple over when she's dried out. You do all the right things and feel satisfied. Then you see an old man on the quay – looking at you. He always looks the same. He'll have a box on wheels and a wagging head which signals a perpetual negative, and what with the peak of his cheese-cutter scything to and fro and his gums champing away he looks like a working model of a combine harvester.

There was a time when we went in for a scrub on a spring tide. She's a tall boat and, dried out, she looks like a bad case of refraction or maybe a long man in a tail suit. She's the only boat with a boot topping that needs arch supports, so we have to be careful.

We moved Harry's bedding, which gave her a nice list, and then we settled down to wait. Inside ten minutes we had an old man who looked as if he'd been left over from Hallowe'en, six yachtsmen all narrowing their eyes and sighting along their thumbs, and a harbour official who stood biting his lip. In addition to that lot there were the trippers explaining to each other what they thought we were. Harry appeared on deck and they all sucked in their breath, he shot back again blushing coyly. We opened the skylight half an inch, and there they all were peering over the edge of the quay like a mantlepiece full of ornaments.

The old man began belting our masthead line with his barrow. I went on deck. 'Bad place to lie 'ere is,' he said, wagging away. 'Meself I'd be 'appier with a leg out.'

He had a complexion like a beach ball. I told him to lay off and then, to show my indifference, I vaulted lightly down into the cockpit and caught my chin on the hatch. It sounded like the lid of a poor-box slamming shut.

I got a nut on a string and tried plumbing a bulkhead crack. It hung the wrong way. Harry was peering up through the navel pipe at his audience. All this time the tide was falling fast and the keel was beginning to crunch on the bottom. It sounded like poor relations working through the crisps at a wedding breakfast. 'I think we'll have a little stroll along the quay and look at her,' I said in a shrill, controlled voice. By the time he'd watered his hair back and polished his teeth with a finger in a fold of his guernsey, we were drying fast.

We went up whistling airily. The audience had doubled. 'I'd have a leg out,' Hallowe'en said. The yachtsmen said good morning and went on sighting.

Harry broke first. He feverishly tied his pipe on the end of a bit of marline and leaned out over the quay. I hung on to his braces and looked away abstractedly.

He should have used more thread on those buttons . . .!

It's a strain all round

There's more to laying up than blowing down the teapot spout and clapping a bean tin over the stove pipe

A stranger, native of some distant inland steppe, and watching a family laying-up fatigue as it approaches in the rain and out of the yard gate, might be forgiven his mistaken outburst of indignation.

'Poor homeless devils,' he thunders brokenly. 'Is there then no justice in the land?'

First comes father under three mattresses – an armadillo in gum boots crowned by flogging plastic sheet; mother comes next, bearing a basin piled high with the pathetic trivia of the galley, and wearing around her neck a lifebuoy which bears the mocking legend *Ecstasy IV*. In the rear is 'our big-lad'; six foot of kneecap, neck and rib cage, thin as workhouse gruel and carrying a load of scatter cushions as if they were kentledge ballast.

They reach the car and the boot is locked.

These final stages of a laying-up party are usually fraught

with passion and drama: there is the matter of the cardboard carton. Designers of these containers make no allowance for the testing circumstances of laying-up. Loaded with steering compass, three bottles of Bass, the log book, a rocket, 25 virginal code flags and a 'Q' which looks like a dog blanket, its bomb doors open at the top of the ladder and father (below) runs out of voice on a piccolo note.

'Nobody told me,' complains our big boy.

The exhortations of yachting magazines imply that the average owner runs shrieking to his fireside at the first touch of frost. 'Fit out for winter – lay up for spring' they howl, explaining how. 'What about your inadequate vents?' they chide, wagging a reproving finger, 'Your cockpit drains spell trouble' they add, spelling it. The owner, unmoved by these threats, grubs around in the galley, sorting out left-overs with an eye to economy. There is the little matter of half a jar of salmon and shrimp paste thrown out by mother. He has been downright bad tempered since breakfast and 'I-don't-know-what-gets-into-you-these-days Bernard.'

'Sheer waste', he says, addressing the fire extinguisher on the bulkhead. 'You'd think it grew on trees!' This theory wins further support upon closer inspection. He eats it for lunch in an awful silence, watched critically and not without ghoulish expectation by his family.

The winter cover is unrolled to reveal spiders of prodigeous size wearing shaggy Harris Tweed pyjama suits. They dash around aimlessly like a Grand Opera crowd scene as the cover is hauled into position, and bolt gratefully through last year's unmended rips and tears, ('Oh I've got a little job for you Florence'). Father crawls along the deck looking for his gas-lighter while the family, in the car, watch the animated canvas convulsions without joy.

Old Harry simplifies the problem of covers which flog in the wind by owning an ex-Goods Yard torp'lin of such admirable tarry stiffness that it has to be unfolded with a crowbar; once in position on deck, the edges are hammered down round the toerail like the crust of some monstrous pie which has been sixty years in the baking and would flatten the appetite of a vulture. Old Harry's smack, abandoned by a generation of fishermen who could pump or fish but not manage both at once, has a counter which hangs down like a dhoti, boasts more sprung butts than the beginner's class at a riding school, and has more lead tingles on her than a church roof. He lays up in Slaughterhouse gully.

This delectable berth, his by common consent, looks like a stage representation of Flander's mud and is infested with every form of blight from teredo to barber's itch. It is cluttered with so many old bicycle wheels that one might suppose the Tour de France to have been confronted suddenly by a quagmire before there was time to stop. At night that mud glows. With the tide out it mutters and gobbles like a club secretary proposing a vote of thanks.

A lesser ship than Old Harry's would be riddled like a meringue inside a week, but that mud and its baleful tenants is powerless against the staunch defence of his gribble.

A nice easy motion

The dicy dart and the deep sea roll

The narrow confines of the modern yacht, plus a motion like trying to get dirt off a shovel, has done much to rob us of the fine rolling shore-gait which should be our heritage. Anyone who watched the mob come ashore after the Fastnet will have been struck by this. Taking their first uneasy

steps with the pessimism of men in hired morning trousers, they waddled gingerly off up the quay as though confronted by a freshly scrubbed hall floor and an uncertainty about what they might have trodden in.

By contrast, the dignity of Old Harry's bearing when ashore is a direct result of a lifetime of bigger and more stately craft with a motion like waterlogged hassocks. With a heel-and-toe shuffle that occupies more pavement space than a barrow load of sofas, his progress goes unadmired by fellow pedestrians. Absorbed as they are in evasive footwork, like folkdancers learning a new set, they have a straight choice of making a dicy dart between those flailing juggernauts and taking uncertain refuge in a shop devoted to the needs of mothercraft.

At sea, motion below-decks brightens the parchment cheek with many a flush of merriment as galloping watch-mates meet sturdy bulkhead with sickening impact. In the heads, where Percy is pumping the flush to cover the clandestine rush of fresh water from the wash-basin, a sudden wild lurch confounds him. Grabbing at the knob of the owner's private locker he is treated to a salvo of unguents, a crepe bandage which makes for the pan like a liberated otter, and a first aid manual open at a picture of a patient sneering at his Potts fracture as if he'd won it in a cracker.

With a following wind and a quartering sea, relaxation for the watch below is at best an intermittent affair. At intervals the resting mariners are granted a view of the cockpit with the boom stuck up like a bottle brush and the helmsman's fists paddling spokes as if he was trying to juggle with empties.

'Watch it!' everybody roars, sitting bolt upright.

A resentful snarl from the cockpit is cut off short as the ship goes into a broach, slamming the spinnaker inside out with a crack that rings the sailmaker's till four hundred miles away. From the bunks haggard faces rear up again like nestlings begging to be fed.

'He's got no idea at all!' they confide, working their eyebrows up and down.

They settle to their health-giving rest again, relaxed as airline passengers studying a slack nut.

It takes more than a half-dozen scatter cushions and a bowl of Brazil nuts to spread a little cheer below-decks when the watch is trying to dress. There is a particular malignancy about a ship in a sea. She waits for trousers to be hauled half-way up and for heads to be securely muffled in the half-donned smock, and then lets got with a heave that sends men bounding to and fro like infants practising music and movement exercises. Under the table we find Percy sorting boots.

To see how the modern crew can adapt to the motion on decks, we have but to watch a foredeck party at work. At the onset of emergency all rush forward, pausing only to unclip their safety harnesses. They swarm round the foot of the mast as if massing for migratory flight, and begin slapping each other's hands off the halliards. All then stagger to the pulpit and back calling loudly for spikes, spanners and sail tiers while the owner, taking the tenor part, brings the show to its moving finale by flinging open the forehatch. Old Harry, suspended by a safety harness of his own contrivance which only lacks a nosebag and crupper, hurtles through to hang there swimming strongly and calling sternly for a heaving line.

The dining car steward who times his delivery of jam sauce for the next tunnel and dribbles it all down your Agatha Christie, has nothing on Old Harry for adapting his roll to the social graces. Leading his little party across a restaurant floor, I have seen him bow graciously to the company after straddling a potted palm with one boot and an ice-bucket with the other. Only the presence behind him of a lady violinist in a black sequinned hold-all and busy with Merrie England ruined what might have been a moment of old world charm. Oblivious to the harpoon thrusts of her bow, she had him off his mark like a runaway horse-rake. Taking in a trolly-load of spirit stove and *crêpes Suzette*, he made a dramatic exit via the pay-desk to a roar of nostalgic applause.

A basin of fun

'It won't be long now,' laughs father, fisting the spokes . . .

No lock-keeper who has suffered the exploratory jab of a yachtsman's boathook can be expected to tug his forelock with the rapidity deemed proper by our forefathers. Nowadays the rising water level in the lock brings into view a plethora of pudding fenders and bobble caps enlivened by the parry and thrust of boathook and mop. The lock keeper watches with the glum resignation of a diner surveying an unusually unappetising *hors d'oeuvres*.

The inland yachtsman who can nip into a lock with the silent dispatch of a hotel guest bagging a bathroom has our admiration though. Not for him the dry mouth of fear and the helmsman's cloistered silence. Alarm is absent from the scene, save for an occasional matron straightening up smartly, alert for mischief at the cry of:

'Give her a touch astern.'

See the British yachtsmen circling gravely outside some French lock, waiting for opening time. Tension is in the air. Apart from looking each other up in Lloyd's and exchanging distant nods they make no other side of frivolity. Our typical owner reads the appropriate passage in the Pilot Book for the sixth time, with his mind a complete blank. Ashore, signals are whooping up and down the signal mast (conspic) and numbers, balls and flags rise and fall with sickening regularity. Some wit calls 'Bingo.' The sally is met with deep breathing silence.

The gates begin to open. Like a hound from the slips our frail bark tears for the widening gap. Relief shows in many a face.

'It won't be long now,' laughs father, fisting the spokes.

He returns a gay wave to the figure in faded blue denims who is dancing and howling on the lock wall – the steamer emerges from the lock with towering bow-wave!

He is brought lower by his ultimate entry to the lock. With a following gale of wind and his engine battling full astern he sweeps into the gap. His offered heaving line is stonily ignored by the faded denim platoon on the wall.

'*Alors, alors,*' they cry at this professional gesture.

'Com-on, com-on, mek queek!'

Father 'meks queeker' than he has ever made before, but it is not until his bow is a ship's length from the far end gate that a ticker-tape exchange of heaving lines (gay carnival touch this) brings him up.

Old Harry uses locks as if they were some sort of mammoth spring trap engineered specially for his down-fall. Deaf to the curses of outgoing traffic, he steers an undeviating course down the middle of the lock. He lowers craggy brows, saltier than a cocktail snack, to the blue dancers on the wall, and the shaken hand of refusal makes no odds to him when he is ready to deliver his heaving line.

'For voo!' he roars, letting go with a two stone coil of wet sisal. The lock attendant stopping this lot between the shoulder blades can count himself lucky to rise again with no worse than a concertinered honker.

It is an interesting feature of design that Old Harry's hooker with the bowsprit run out, exactly spans the width of the average lock. This demonstration usually follows an engine failure half-way in and Harry, satisfied that his ship is secure in this position, lifts the engine cover and peers in as if if were a raree-box filled with drolleries. Heedless of the howling mob he gives himself up to the art and science of mechanics.

Men have been winkled out of their quay-side sentry boxes by that questing spar, and the Dutch courtesy flag flown by Old Harry irrespective of port nationality does little to restore them to laughing good humour. Port officials have resigned from responsible positions at the mere sight of Old Harry's vessel on the horizon and, as the rising-water level in the lock brings his eyebrows above the edge, we have seen strong men falter and fall back crying aloud their old mothers' names.

Once in the basin a berth must be chosen. Father's repeated cry of 'Ahoy there! Have you got a baarth for me?'

brings only a puzzled shrug from the berthing master. Our boat will bring up alongside a huge Italian motor yacht, people by men in linen caps all stumbling around in dark glasses. Mother immediately begins sewing little curtains for the fo'c's'le porthole.

With Old Harry safely inside the basin and the trap sprung behind him, stern determination gives way to the beaming benevolence which he reserves for foreigners and which serves as a substitute for speech.

He will select a small French cruiser and promptly enmesh it in a web of sisal. The captives are in for forty-eight harrowing hours of Old Harry. He will laugh good-heartedly at their rig, and with commendable tact control his natural mirth at their attempts to speak English. They eventually make their escape filled with tea, richer by one of his own home-made sisal fenders as hard as granite, and poorer by the price of ten tickets for a club raffle – prize, a bottle of Australian tonic wine.

Scavengers o' the seas

No true cruising yachtsman can sail past a patch of flotsam without a covetous gleam in his eye

If the day ever dawns when I see a real cruising yachtsman sail straight past an empty paint drum without making a grab for it, I'll go straight ashore, stand my sailing trousers in a corner and take to my shawl and gruel. I've yet to see your true all-wool cruising yachtsman who could resist a spot of flotsam or jetsam. I've watched a cruiser race disintegrate as if a salvo had been fired at it, and all because the leaders ran into a patch of seaweed laced with a few choice noggings of two-by-four.

Incidentally it's an odd thing about the timber you see floating at sea. It always looks knot-free, planed and varnished and yet, when you get it aboard, it's bristling with

great bent nails like a spinster's scullery and looks as if it had been hewn with a bread saw.

The lure of the scavenger begins ashore. Take any owner you like. He may have just paid a sixty quid yard bill and be enjoying the sunshine of the manager's smile but, as they stroll together through the boatbuilding shop, this fact won't prevent him from grabbing a half-handful of brass screws from among the shavings on the floor when nobody's watching. Once at sea he'll revert to the flint-eyed marauder, scourge o' the seas from whom no oil-drum, broken oar, deflated cork fender or biscuit tin is safe. Seagulls and the cruising yachtsman between them keep our coasts clean and pleasant.

Cork fenders rank high as spoils in this harvest of the sea. One visualizes great ships far at sea hurling out huge rope sausages with Olympian prodigality, and inshore grim little bands of determined yachtsmen, waiting for them to float in, stiffening their thews in readiness. I've seen them come with their thews so stiff that they needed only a twist of wisteria around their demenures to look like the old garden gate. These fenders are of unsurpassed pleasure to capture, being full of handy bights and stray ends, but once on deck they subside like auntie after the Food Fair. They also give off a spreading pool of foul juice made gay by the jerking antics of small marine life – later they live on peevishly dribbling granulated cork and sand. Once a fender comes aboard you're stuck with it.

It's the glass fishing float that stands supreme prize in the game. I've seen healthy-minded men with their eyes bright with the fever of desire punting one of those things across the Channel with a boat hook in a nightmare snooker tournament – unable to get it aboard and determined to have it at all costs. The deck bucket is a favourite tackle. While father tacks, gybes and howls directions his crew hurl themselves from rail to rail pointing and gibbering. All this is excused as being 'good man-overboard drill', but the man who falls over on one side as a glass float appears on the other would be well advised to start trudgeoning.

Old Harry lays modest claim to having one of the finest collections of Brasso tins around the coast, and it's half a grapefruit to a sack of corks that his best cap came from Cowes via the last of the ebb from Portsmouth Dockyard. It is said that anything exceeding ten feet in length is the business of HM Receiver of Wrecks. You'll have HM's Officer – all cap and trouser-clips waiting around on shore, mildly curious to know why Old Harry should wear his ankle length storm front and chose to walk sideways dribbling down the pontoon. It's like the Trinity House boys say; 'You just can't put a thing down!'

A bone in her teeth

The advent of the marine speedometer has spelt *finis* to the social gaiety of the cockpit. Where once the helmsman held laughing court with an audience spellbound at his sparkling rhetoric bleak silence reigns. No schoolboy carpenter notes the application of set-square to his mortise joint with more foreboding than does the helmsman eyeing the tell-tale clock.

'I think the wind must have taken off a shade,' hazards our Percy trying to account for the flagging needle. 'I had her up to ten a few minutes ago!'

The owner, who knows you couldn't get her up to ten knots on a handcart and down a cliff face, treats this claim with naked disbelief and takes up his stance abaft the wheel. Percy's ears light up like lift buttons and he begins using the spokes as if he were juggling with dumb-bells.

The comforting knowledge that no boat can be shoved along faster than her designed speed under sail provides blessed relief for many a half-hearted owner, half-heartedly pressed by his crew to set the spinnaker.

'Well I'm as keen as the next man,' he states accurately 'and I'd say, "yes" in a flash if it would help.'

They all sigh with relief, boom out the genoa and congratulate each other on a wise and advantageous move.

Old Harry, comfortable in the theory that the more you stick up the faster you'll go, reaches his designed maximum four and a half knots under jumbo and bonnet thereafter rolling up the sea ahead of him like a piano on a rag rug.

'Let's see if we can put a bone in her teeth,' he offers, setting a jackyard topsail, a Jimmy Green and a reeking marquee of cotton. Immediately a great hole yawns under her quarter and she squats back in it like a punctured ballcock.

The art of enjoying a slow boat is never to sail in company with a faster one. Witness the little family cruiser with a midship section like a tin chapel.

'Look, she's going like a train!' chants the delighted owner, innocent of ironical reference to her fitful and laboured progress. The rub comes when a strange sail heaves in sight. Elated to the point of belligerence he gives chase at once. A short while later, gazing stiffly away from her receding transom, he begins to feel like last man in a father's day sack race.

'Those things are all right if you don't mind discomfort,' he jeers, darting a look of newly-awakened disgust at his own spacious coachroof.

The speedometer, reading as optimistically as a holiday camp brochure, has brought sail trimming to a pitch of refinement which leaves no time for the helmsman's mate to brood down the open hatch on the little cameo of comfort below. Simulating keenness at half-hourly intervals for the benefit of any wakeful brass who may be listening, he gives the genoa sheet a couple of pawls and cries out in triumph, thereafter checking it back to where it was before, a little deception condoned by the yawning helmsman.

The true enthusiast is the real menace. An encouraging response from the needle fires him to trim out the last vestige of weather helm. The traditionalist, raised in an age when weather helm was thought as essential to windward work as sulphur and treacle to establishing healthy thoughts in the young, is left feeling as if he were steering a tot's fire-engine in a funfair, and begins making a course like an Ouija board.

Relief comes only with the fouling of the pitot, a calamity closely associated with the anglers on Cherbourg inner mole (*'Eh! eh! eh! eh! Attention!'*). As the needle plunges dramatically to zero and frantic knuckles hammer on the glass, I have seen racing owners assailed by gloomy doubt like the purchaser of a postal bargain duffle coat watching it come through the letter box.

The dinghy man, his pants skimming the water in a ten-knot plane, regards speed as his personal prerogative and bitterly resents it when displayed by any other craft. The runabout owner hounded out to sea by dripping Harbour Master and waved farewell by the pedalling feet of pram dinghy oarsmen, is as popular with dinghy sailors as a scratching dog under a tea-trolley.

'Places changed rapidly,' scribble yachting correspondents busily as the curling wash wreaks its havoc among the leaders, while diapered trapeze crews hover on beating pinions. It takes the arrival of Old Harry with a following wind and a jammed halliard to restore good humour and order. With his sucking wake already tenanted by a pedalo, a selection of beach balls and a sunbather on a Li-Lo, lucky are the helmsmen who come within its foaming orbit.

Don't give him biscuits

– or anything else. Helmsmen are on a plane above (or below) ordinary mortals

Silly to relate, but I once gave a biscuit to a helmsman! Gentle reader may smile, perhaps – in fact, he may laugh his great chuckle-head off at such naïvety, but I was a simple country lad with sacking round my legs in those days and I had a frank, open countenance like a candidate for an endowment policy. Mentally as thick as two short planks – *and I hadn't raced before.*

I didn't know that a helmsman is in *purdah.* He's a sort of broody hen. With all the rest of the crew squawking up and down the deck having fun, he must sit with a faintly striken look on his face, as if he were listening to a Prom (with the neighbours watching). You see that same frowning and slightly indignant expression worn by those week-end Tarzans in  swimming pools, who practise abdominal isolation and flex things at the deep end.

The owner fought for oxygen. He said, shaking his head and laughing his disbelief. 'You gave him a *biscuit.* DON'T give him biscuits. *I* couldn't eat a biscuit and race!'

My own mouth was too full to reply. All I could manage was a dispirited little puff of dust.

Now get this right. Your helmsman is on a separate plane. If he can really steer a straight course, so much the better, but his real task is to preserve this doleful expression and hold the wheel still every time the owner looks at him. In light airs he should purse the lips and sneer gently up at the sails. At five minute intervals he should cut icily into any conversation that's going on and say, 'Perhaps someone would like to have a look at my genny,' an invitation which, in any other circle might be treated with alarm but, on a yacht racing offshore, can be relied upon to send huge men scuttling up the deck to gaze accusingly at the headsail.

At night, when the watch feels a bit matier, things tend to relax. The rumble of conversation goes on intermittently and interminably – like the man who just beats you to the telephone kiosk. Don't let it fool you, though, we haven't reckoned with the navigator.

Some time during the night he's going to rise from his

roost black of heart and bleary, and he is going to begin D F navigating. He glares at the chart and then at the deck-log, hoping to find discrepancies. That done, he puts on his earphones and pokes his head up into the cockpit. In the ear-phones he looks like Demon Dirt coming out of a crack in the sink.

'Well, you see, there was Jayne Mansfield and this revolving door . . .' the helmsman is explaining.

'When-you-are-on-say-ON!' The navigator enunciates with rude deliberation. 'I'll say NOW and you say ON.'

At the promise of this bleak little conversation-to-come, the helmsman is suddenly spurred to frenzied activity. Wildly, he begins to saw at the wheel. His bottom lip is stuck out like a glue ladle, and he is surrounded by an aura of guilt – guilt-edged, as one might say.

From being a mere five or ten degrees off course and on either side, the helmsman will now begin to put the ship into a series of dizzy swoops back and forth across the course. He sees the lubber line as an elusive little beetle. The card roars past it.

'ON,' he yells fractionally late. 'ON – just a minute – ON – ON. Oh, hell – ON – ON. Ah – hang on. No, that wasn't . . . ON – that was.'

The navigator reappears. 'What *average* course can you make?' he asks. He then disappears without waiting for an answer.

Six minutes later it is the same. The card hurtles past the lubber line under the helmsman's frantic hand and 'ON' he shrieks. His voice is carried away on the wind. 'ON . . . ON, ononon,' like a little grey soul wandering in limbo. The navigator, for his trouble, gets a cocked hat like Barnum's Big Top, or he plots a line which goes wandering aimlessly and inexplicably off into the dark Atlantic.

There is a wheel-jargon which varies very little from ship to ship.

For instance – 'Like to take her for a bit?' freely translated means 'It's damn cold and blowing like a station booking office with the door open.' It also means that you're going to be stuck with that wheel for the rest of the watch unless you use the 'Hang-on-to-her-while-I-get-another-sweater-on' gambit.

'She's yawing a bit now and then,' is a remark which should be made for the benefit of the owner who has taken an interest in the wake. It really means that you can't hold the slab-sided sentry box, and the liquid in the compass is other than alcohol. On the other hand, though she may be steering like a runaway tea-trolley at the time, when you hand over you should exclaim (as the card swoops past the course).

'Right, then. Steering herself. Oh, five, five.' You get the hell out of it and leave the new wheel to sort it out in frenzied silence, for he can't own up to finding it difficult after that.

In the days of kindly ships which went straight, your helmsman on a coasting ketch might have to hand the topsail, stay the ship round, pump the bilge and brew tea for the old man. Nowadays, there's no hope of mumbling even a raisin. Just the same, there's a harrowing account about the man who had a stopwatch in one hand and a biscuit in the other. 'Five, four, three, two,' he counted. Then there was a pause as he spat out a hair-spring . . . 'one, GUN,' he added. The owner, oblivious to this little drama, was steering. Haggard with enjoyment, whimpering like a ratting terrier, he allowed himself a quick glance. '*I* couldn't win a race and eat a watch,' he said crossly.

Odd aspects

TAKE A SALTY CONVERSATION between two cruising yachtsmen in a buffet car: 'We picked up this little nunn for the night in the Blackwater' says one of them. A nervous parson nearby waves aside the cheeseboard and departs in haste, leaving a tip that cripples his stipend. That's an *odd aspect*, otherwise this heading is a bare faced excuse for lumping together all the stuff that's left over.

The best policy

... adventures and perils ...

If you could see your insurance agent on a Monday morning after a week-end blow, the cry of 'They must be rolling in it' would fall less readily to your lips. With the 'phone held six inches from his ear, squarking its twenty minute solo of scrupulous seamanship in the face of overpowering odds, the little depth-charges, daggers and skulls which he doodles on his blotter might be easier to forgive. If they rang the Lutine Bell every time a yacht came to rest across a sewer outfall, it would be hammering away like a bent tail-shaft.

The Underwriters lying moaning in their sleep, dream of the adventures and perils which, so the policy says, '. . . they are contented to bear . . .' Meanwhile, our mariners are severally engaged in poking the exploratory boathook at a prop shaft which wears a muffler of two inch combination rope, spelling out 'WHAT AM I' in morse to a fascinated Spanish trawler, or collecting incriminating specimens of paint scrapings in a match box.

The deathless prose of an owner's report must make heady

reading for those lucky clerks. Composed on some lofty perch ('While it's still fresh in my mind dear') the economy of style would make a bank statement seem verbose by comparison. 'During the period preceding contact . . .' runs the report, 'I observed the vessel to be navigating without caution . . .' Put baldly, there was old dad shimmering like a mirage over an over-heated engine and yelling 'Is it coming out yet?' to a non-commital row of buttocks lining the side above the cooling water outlet.

A traditional behaviour-pattern binds the British yachtsman on such occasions. Face to face and swopping agents or peering out through the hole in the topsides like newly awakened hibernates, our protagonists keep up a shaky façade of composure. The offender must examine the damage with professional understanding, while the injured party protests happily that it could have happened to anyone, old man. It is no easy role. With your pulpit stuck up in the air like a praying mantis or some clumsy squelch fighting a losing battle between holding up elastic-waisted pyjamas and frenzied attempts to take the wilt out of your buckled bumkin ('That'll straighten out OK old man . . .'), it requires a high degree of facial control to jack up the moustache in a grimace of smiling good-fellowship.

It is no sixth sense which warns the prowling longshoreman of impending lolly. The sight of a yachtsman drifting up on a fast ebb and nipping in and out of his wheelhouse faster than a dining-car steward flogging tickets for the second lunch, plus an exhaust pipe spitting five-sixteenths nuts and washers, is all that it takes to call him to horse. The conscientious owner knows better than to let on that he's insured though. His babbled denials accompanied by crossed fingers, carry about as much conviction as his attempts to account for the half-gallon of anti-fouling that he used to stick on his Schedule A house maintenance claims.

A yachtsman offshore and lacking in both wind and petrol may also need his wits about him. Our 'toilers of the deep', hastily forsaking their fishing grounds in their anxiety to tell him that he's in a 'nasty 'ole spot Capting, and how about a tow in?' are reluctant to have their efforts labelled as 'assistance' rather than salvage. What with the great hairy hand clamped on his tiller and the drifter beating the pistons out of her pots in an effort to part the tow and substitute one of her own lines, our man is to be forgiven for his fears. It soon becomes obvious that a firm handshake, five pints of bitter and 'A little something to buy the wife a new hat, haw, haw' is not going to bring about an embarrassing show of gratitude. The introductory huffing and blowing heard over the insurance agent's 'phone, is due warning of the identity of the man at the other end.

Old Harry, having gathered from a study of his policy that '. . . enemies, pirates, rovers and thieves' beset him on all sides, regards the rest of the maritime world with lowering suspicion. His reports of each fresh brush with the foe leave him portrayed as a stern upholder of law sailing perilously among maritime morons. His telephone voice is a hot-buttered-scone bellow maintained with some effort, as if he doubted the effectiveness of the instrument beyond normal hailing range. In a 'legalese' proper to the occasion he reports his latest incidents.

His account of how 'the aforementioned pier-head slot machine, flying no signals, extended beyond the line of my bowsprit', leaves no doubt about which of these fixtures was the transgressor, but it does no justice to the harrowing scene which actually took place, or of the Piermaster, dancing among the wreckage, who trod on a stray liquorice torpedo from the shattered machine and measured his length on the deck while Old Harry was absorbed in confirming what the butler saw.

All change

The yachtsman ashore – modes and methods of transport

The inland yachtsman en route by rail for his natural element presents the casual traveller with a sharp impression of the rude seafaring life. Knees are drawn smartly

aside as he blunders into the compartment loaded with essential stores.

'There, then,' he comments to a watchful and hostile company, 'I think she'll ride all right.'

He hefts a mottle grip on to the rack where it lodges with the insecurity of a top hat at a chapel wedding. The passenger seated beneath has nice time in which to open his packed lunch and commence that sidelong munching peculiar to railway carriage refreshment, before it leaps down on him like a wounded panther avenging its mate.

The offshore racing man who rides in the dining car and wears his back hair curling over his collar may excite little notice, but the week-end cruising man causes as much speculation as a clip-on bow tie found floating in the gravy boat.

Clutching a biscuit tin sardonically labelled 'Good Time Assortment' (and which contains a home-made pork pie calculated to line the lee rail like the start of the hundred yard free style), he carries more kit than a plumber's mate. He stands an outboard in the corridor which leaves a puddle and causes a ticket inspector, all greatcoat, wattle and nostril, to banish a widow and her pooch to the guard's van.

The Sunday night return of exhausted sportsmen offers an even grimmer spectacle.

'Don't look at him, dear,' urge mothers to their young, measuring their distance from the communication cord.

After a week-end of sore trial and five pints at the bar, our mariner is no sight for the squeamish. Stacked in a corner like a job lot at a jumble sale, and lower jaw resting on his chest as decoratively as the firebox door of a bogey stove, he rolls up his eyes and emits a succession of gobbling snores.

There are those who merit no pity, of course. Any ocean race which ends up far from home after a cobbly two days sees this guilty little migration.

'I feel awful having to leave you ... but you know the boss! ! !' they mourn happily, legging it for plane or train. Later, flying over grey and troubled sea where returning Class III plunges and staggers in the same hole like gum-booted farmers at a wet agricultural show, they suck their regulation boiled sweet with relish and note the busy traffic of oilskinned figures 'twixt rail and companion.

While travel by public transport is no hardship to the man who enjoys being identified as a yachtsman and only takes his cap off for a haircut, there are moments of discomfort. With more brass buttons than a horsehair sofa he may look more nautical than a novelty bottle opener, but it only needs some elderly PO with a jaw like a brick privvy to sit opposite and our gay friend wilts like a posy in a timekeeper's office.

Old Harry, who runs no such risks, prefers to travel in the guard's van anyway. Reasoning that he gets a longer ride, this Spartan choice enables him to guard his own kit. Like Gordon at Khartoum he sits surrounded by these knobbly ramparts while porters howl and gesticulate without. Sitting easily on a crate of Buff Orpingtons, he offers valuable geographical advice on the consignment of packages, a service which ultimately results in a retired parson at Liphook finding himself recipient of a calf in a sack, and an elderly spinster at Woking dropping lucky for the crate of lavatory pans. They never know their donor.

'I think you've got it'

The urge to instruct beginners carries its own reward

It is a strange belief held by every yachtsman that he is a born teacher, of the art of sailing anyway. 'You'll jolly soon pick it up,' he tells the beginner with laughing condescension, beginning to sketch out a parallelogram of forces with the stem of his pipe. The tyro, who stands with one wet finger stuck up in the air glances at it and smiles sottishly. 'Mind you,' the yachtsman goes on, 'I have my own method, which even a baby in arms could grasp.'

We've seen these methods. They can take the form of a

three-hour exposition with blackboard and chalk which is as heavy with threat as a Victorian gas geyser, or they can degenerate into a sail round the bay to the accompaniment of a high-pitched nasal whine, punctuated by cries of naked terror.

The beginner, distinguishable by the fluttering price tag on the neck of his windcheater and the ineffectual little paddling motion of his hands as he blunders around trying to look as though he's helping rig the boat, is a sitting duck for these dons of the jigger stick. If he scorns to learn by the orthodox methods, he is faced with joining the ranks of the self-taught, to be seen poling painfully along the lee side of the shallows with drooping booms and luffs hanging in bights like the gardener's trousers.

The learner will have studied 'the book' of course. He is ready to believe that he will be pursued wherever he goes by that damning little dotted line, and he has noted the diagrams featuring boat 'A' and boat 'B', in which 'A' is handled by a prig of nauseating skill and 'B' blunders from one catastrophe to the next with heart-warming realism. 'The book' is no preparation for what actually happens.

First he must learn to move around in the boat with confidence. He steps gingerly aboard with distrust written large on his twitching features, like a housewife mounting the chemist's scales, and seats himself hard up against the tiller. The instructor licks his lips and draws breath.

There are several ways of instilling the mechanics of the art. Some favour a rigged boat on a trailer ashore, in which our novice sits like a poor man's Queen o' the May under the wondering gaze of some half-score of trippers, and is swivelled around until he cries for quarter. Others are all for getting afloat and 'giving him the tiller at once' – a little gift which is rarely accepted with gratitude. The instructor crouches amidships and keeps up a commentary on each fresh disaster, aiming to make the whole thing sound like a frolic in the hay. They go down-wind in a series of shattering gybes, and the pupil, who is in imminent danger of being trepanned, is concerned only with an animal urge for self-preservation.

'You're beginning to get it!' The instructor howls, between urgent huffs at his inflator jacket. Seconds later they are exploring the wonderland of the sea-bed.

Some instructors, who enjoy the controlled modulations of their own voices, keep up a steady babble of advice, explanation and prayer, others sit in monumental silence, it is their method and they have told the pupil to 'carry on as if I wasn't here'. They are about as self-effacing as a bathroom tenor in a plaster-board flatlet.

Many men attempt to teach their wives to sail, but they are sitting on a china egg from the word go. Wives will renounce the theories at once, re-invent the boat inside the first ten minutes and remark tartly that 'other men seem to look different in shorts . . .' A wife will let the plate down on her husband's fingers and then, as he is fighting for altitude, she'll tell him that she wishes he'd try to show a little control!

You will see them go drifting by on the ebb talking in low and animated tones through their teeth . . . 'I'm not an animal!' . . . you hear – they break off to wrinkle a smile at you and drift on. 'All I said was . . .' comes the time-old cry as they continue the lesson.

It is a rewarding game, and many yachtsmen actually volunteer their services to clubs and holiday schemes. They have to take the luck of the game. The instructor may have had his eye to a long and conscientious course of instruction with the leopard-skin blonde with the built-in pout, but he's more like to drop in for the beldame in the divided skirt and brown sandshoes with the figure like an articulated lamp.

She will be passed fit to sail solo in the second lesson, which only goes to show!

Trousery look
Cut and fit is all

I can recall a time when it was possible to buy a pair of jeans for *working in*.

You may laugh but that is a fact! There were shops which sold working gear and you could buy a nice stiff pair of jeans, pressed flat as a farmer's Sunday cap and as innocent of brass stars, comic stitching and tin zips as a Bishop's gaiters, and with *legs* instead of attenuated tubes.

You could put your hands in the patch pockets without bending double to get a bit of slack. You had a bit of room in the tail-pieces too. They didn't fit so tight you had to walk on tip-toe, and they came with a great label sewn on the rump like a prize-winning Aberdeen Angus. They were in fact PANTS. There was only one colour – a nice freckled blue. They were neither pre-shrunk, pre-faded nor were they recommended by television cowboys.

I went looking for jeans the other day and I knew just what I wanted. Harry had recommended his tailor to me. It was one of those bulging shops which have a thicket of flying jackets and mess-tins, Balaclava helmets and flame-throwers festooning the frontage like the seaweed at low water springs. They had always given Harry first class service, he told me. Any pillar box could have worn Harry's suits with distinction so that didn't meant a lot.

To get in there you needed a bush knife and a marching compass, both of which were thoughtfully on sale. I forced aside a camp bed and parted a frieze of as-new-pants-cellular and confronted the tailor. He looked as shifty an old rogue as ever gripped a slack fold. If his eyes had been any closer together and his beak any sharper he would have looked like a pair of forceps. I said I wanted some wide-legged jeans.

He gave me a very gentle smile. His head panned to and fro like an electric fan. 'If you was to offer me fifty nicker, in my hand – now – I couldn't do you a wide guv. There's no call. They're out. Now I can do you a "Pancho" or a "Waggoner" or a "Puncher" which is all styled, prefaded and calf-shrunk but I can't do the wide. After all,' (he went inside his collar and spread his hands), 'after all I can't sell what I haven't got. I'm only a human bean like anybody elst.'

I tried on the 'Pancho.' I went behind a folding bath and eased into them. All I needed was the eye make-up and a cardboard crossbow to look like an ageing ballet dancer doing Swan Lake. I stalked like a cockerel towards the centre of the floor and then back. He watched. 'Very nice fit,' he said hollowly. I took them off and bought a mess tin instead.

Where are the pants that grand-dad used to wear? This is a generalization only. In fact, we know that grand-dad's pants have been lagging the cistern in the false roof for the past ten years, and a pretty job they made of it too.

Now those were PANTS. None of your synthetic mixtures that grout your hunkers when you trot but WOOL. When they get wet you may reek like a bothy full of highland ewes and steam like a damp hay-stack in the early stages of spontaneous combustion, but they are still warm. Pants like those are a snug fit under the armpits and intimidate people. To get that truly trousery look you have only to top up your braces a shade and cultivate a trick of blocking the companionway.

These corduroy and cotton pants fit nice and easy when you buy them, but once they're wet! I've seen people in cotton pants staggering around stricken, unable to bend a knee. Fall down in pants like that and all you can do is kick – next thing you know there's a constable poking a pencil between your teeth and loosening your collar. You're helpless. The only worse thing is to hitch your suspender belt to your ankle-socks and run for a bus.

With a pair of navvy cords, a mole-skin waistcoat, a wet day and a warm room, you can scatter a miasma that would make a buzzard's nest seem sweet as a posy.

Pastel shades do not interest me, nor siliconization, pasturization, double zipped flibbert nor grip-top gussets. Pants of any shape are an improvement when your shanks look like a rescued greyhound on its hind legs. To assure me that 'everybody is wearing them in Basque yellow' makes me howl for a kilt. Let narrow legs be for old mess-dressed warriors with rheumy eyes and regimental anecdotes, I look like a tuning fork in trews.

One can still buy policemens' trousers of course. There remains only the dark question; why didn't those policemen *want* their trousers any more? I have some unpleasant theories.

A bit of bunting

Yachtsmen are great lads for a flag. From cap to play pants they're peppered with flags like a sand castle competition, but show them a hoist of code and they bring up all-standing as if they'd stuffed the curtains in with their shirt-tails.

'Can't quite make it out from here,' they laugh falsely, screwing up their eyes and staring in frantic incomprehension. Offer them the glasses and the naked venom of their

glance takes you back to the time you dropped the bean-bag in the sixty yard relay.

Yachtsmen like it to be assumed that they babbled their international code at mother's knee but there's always the unlikely chance that the next man *does* know his code. With Reed's in one hand, Stanley on the halliard and all hands sorting flags, they can send you a message a shade faster than you might chip out a reply in granite.

Watch father identifying his class starting flag on regatta day. 'Blue with yellow stripes,' he reads through his binoculars, 'Now lad let's see if you know what it is, eh.' He waits with gritted teeth for the answer and then makes a copy-book start among the Dabchicks.

The time to see him really blossom is on the occasion of his return to the home port after his summer cruise. He determines to 'make his number'. The flags, in disorder since the Queen's Birthday, provide a rousing experience for the spectators in the Watch House. A grizzled old ex-Yeoman with a jaw like a maltster's shovel, translates father's signal in a voice rendered unsteady by deep emotion. 'I am an airship,' he decodes. 'Do you require boiler water? I have picked up telegraph cable with my anchor. I require a dirt boat.'

The matter of Morse is no better. 'I'm afraid my Morse is getting a bit rusty,' with a rueful laugh.

It's rustier than a Moslem's corkscrew. There was a time when, as members of the Peewit Patrol, they could send an alphabet the length of the church hut – now we watch them staggering around the saloon taking radio fixes with the Heron. 'Da-di-di-di-dah-di', they chant hopefully. It sounds like a crossed trunk line during Cowes Week.

The sight of the furious flicker of light from the harbour entrance has a stimulating effect upon the whole ship's company. Father takes soundings, starts the engine, consults Channel Pilot and shines a light on his sail number as if he thought it might win him a prize. Safe phrases for such occasions, are 'Did anyone get that?' (implying stern rebuke) or 'I'm afraid it was a shade too fast for me' (which hints modestly at an exhibitionist ashore), but the best course is to give a deep professional chuckle as if sharing a technical jest. The odds are that you are watching a distant District Nurse pedalling past the gasworks railings.

Flag etiquette is another matter altogether. Old Harry is very strict about dipping to ships of the Royal Navy, a compliment duly appreciated by ratings as they double along a carrier's flight deck, trip over a bollard and slide to a screaming halt at the foot of the ensign staff. We have seen many a touching little tableau enacted by some subby with crumbs on his quivering chin, standing at the salute while a matelot shins the staff on an urgent errand. Harry's ensign, distinctively defaced by a patch reading 'Produce of Jersey', was acquired along with an assortment of bunting following a high wind at an Agricultural Show.

One of his little conceits is what he calls 'giving 'em a show'. This is a ceremony re-enacted whenever he visits a new port. Pushing up a bow-wave like the Severn Bore his vessel drives unswervingly towards the local yacht club, where the dinghy fleet is just entering the final chorus. His

arm sweeps down and aloft goes a bundle of bag-wash
rejects to break forth in a volume of dust, bottle caps and
moths fighting gamely to return to base. He lays down the
sounding pole with which he has been assisting dinghy
helmsmen to put their boats about, and acknowledges the
cheery waves of the race officers with an old and patriotic
gesture. It would be difficult to find the dry eye on those
occasions!

Bare essentials

The offshore owner bidding for the light-weather stakes,
stripped down to stopwatch and suspenders, filleting the
sardines and floating two inches above his marks has still to
reckon with his crew's kit.

'If you can't pack it – wear
it,' is the motto. You can fool
your owner about the
weight of a bag so long
as you can keep your
eyebrows from vibrating
with concerted effort.
The art lies in swinging
it up over the rail with
seeming indifference at the
same time disguising your
involuntary grunt of hellish
strain by crying 'Hello
there' in an explosion of

tortured lungs. The owner, toes trapped under the bag, gives
a falsetto scream of welcome.

Packed scientifically in the privacy of the home, the canvas
grip can be distended to the limit and the zip drawn over by
the aid of a simple tackle. Only the sponge bag will have
been forgotten and this goes into the pocket of your oily
(lashed on top) to be discovered at midnight as a flattened

pasty of ointment and Brylcreem. The bag with more built-in stresses than a boxed-in bath and humming like a power station is ready for the road. On the train the zip will begin to peel back to base and, like the bursting of some monstrous bud, it will put forth a grisly Airtex blossom before the fascinated gaze of the fellow traveller.

The wise crew, arriving with fingers permanently crooked and an arm of uncanny length like a municipal guide, makes haste to don all spare clothing hitherto carried in separate bundles. Booted and oil-skinned he makes a manly figure in the July heat. The owner sees him from afar.

'Why, here's one of my chaps coming' he laughs proudly. A frown darkens his brow as he notes the lurching gait and the arms extended stiffly from the sides. The launch out to the moorings will be thronged with shifty crews all trying to stand in front of their kit. Early arrivals aboard, having already disguised their own loads, are ready with a welcoming 'Throw me your bag Norman'. This is a mere figure-of-speech, such a missile would face them with a harsh decision, either to leave the ship in a flat racing dive or risk a rib cage.

Once aboard with our little deceit, unobserved, we can seek out a dark corner, trigger off the zip and jump smartly aside – Knee deep in wool and aperients it will be then that the owner will come upon us. Speaking through his nose he will indicate the locker reserved for us. It will be about the size of a triangular boot box with a lid opening on the settee and engineered to spring open at ten minute intervals throughout the race. The only time when this cannot happen is when the navigator (stubble, nobility and wake-me-for-the-forecast) occupies the settee. It would be a stout-hearted man who would brave that sagging jaw and the urgent moans and whimpers of fix-haunted sleep, just to get at his bag of Summer Fruit Selection cont. gluc.

The matter of choosing a sailing bag is of some urgency. From the dinghy sailor in the changing room, standing pinkly by his little tumuli of steaming wool, to the offshore teeth-and-trouser veteran raised on the wet old ships with barnacled binnacles which went under at the Needles and only came up to round the Fastnet, the matter of kit is critical.

There is the air travel bag (with less flying hours than a Galapagos turtle) and an infinite variety of canvas udders produced by sailmakers anxious to use up stocks of duck. There is the kit-bag which exerts a strange gravitational pull on anything sought in a hurry and, inevitably carried by youths with long chins, the cricket bag. Perhaps it is only fitting that Old Harry should have been hailed as the finest exponent of carried kit. I have seen monuments less impressive than Old Harry's.

When Old Harry deposits his huge dun-coloured sack on a station platform you'll see porters circling it warily sparring for an opening, and RSPCA officials trying to feed it with hay. His gladstone is the size of a dog kennel. In the corridor of a fast-moving train his kit-bag assumes even greater proportions. I have seen an old lady fall astride it in her efforts to get past; she had to ride it like a jockey from Liphook to Southsea. The remainder of his gear, containing shaving mug, strop, pomade, bottled Bass and hurricane lanthorn, is carried in a huge canvas howdah on his back. A gift from his tailor at the government surplus stores and a relic of the American Armed Forces, it bears the misleading legend 'Nat Stanwyjski'. Unpacked below decks, the saloon becomes peopled by a ghostly regiment of flannel arms and legs, and waves of camphor pervade the ship. We need only the home-made pickles and a simnel cake to give the Church Hall rebuilding fund a flying start.

Owner or moaner

Pity him for sometimes he has something to complain about

Picture an owner, alone and dispirited, rolling his engine up a plank to get it aboard, like a great, glum dung-beetle in a boiler-suit hefting a mollock of nastiness into its nest – or wherever they put it. This is no exaggeration. This is an OWNER!

The universal dogs-body, the man with the lolly (*sic*). Men with their boats completely and irrevocably in the hands of crews, are owners. If they race, then they are deeper in the moils than even they know.

Crews are all disemboated owners in their own eyes. They have no boat, He has one. They will sail it for him. It's as simple as that. and it's a short step to the state where lips curl gently when the owner makes a statement out loud on his own boat.

With the possible exception of first-timers being given their chance and tearing round the deck coiling down ropes and sirring the owner – with that exception, the rest of them are 'giving old Jack a sail in his own heap'. They have taken over.

Let the owner dare to be late – he's worked until the last moment earning enough dough to justify his sail – his crew are all comfortably settled in, drinking his gin.

'I hope to God he's not late for the start,' one says. A shadow of annoyance (which is like a little plush eye-shade) crosses their faces. 'We *must* be off this mooring at twenty-past, whatever happens.'

'Hope he's remembered to order a new pair of sheet winches.'

'Hope he got the spinnaker repaired.'

'Hope he remembers what I told him about getting a coil of Terylene for the kedge – so much nicer to handle.' ... and so on.

Now why doesn't he come ranting aboard cracking a rhino-hide whip? Why doesn't he 'lend his eye a terrible aspect' and roar, 'Out you damned spots! You flaccid miserable coat-hangers with skin on. On deck, damn you, and get your thieving hooks off my gin'?

He crawls aboard in his comical cap and mumbles 'Sorry I'm late chaps.'

Now there is always a 'Little Specialist' in every crew. He wears a brine-soaked smock which takes up more cockpit room than an Anderson shelter, and he has agreed to sail on this basket. There is also 'The Man From The Crew List' who goes into partnership with the Specialist right away. They convey that they are in some way to be respected. They let fall occasionally names of famous ocean racers and of the derring-do they saw aboard them.

They show a reluctance to wash up.

These two exchange significant glances as the owner outlines his race strategy. 'Yees,' they agree, 'Of course we *could* do that.' They imply that they could also all leap over the side playing musical instruments as the gun goes off.

'I expect the *Cloud* and those chaps will do so-and-so,' they muse . . . 'but we could do what you suggest – skipper.'

At the gun, something like a great, blue, Bermudian-rigged Bentley slashes past, manned by a hawk-faced crew in oilies. 'Sailed on her, Fastnet '77,' Little Specialist notes. 'Not bad, quite handy.'

The owner looks around at his gas pipe stanchions and feels as if he had grubby cuffs at a cocktail party. 'Afraid our old ship doesn't like this point of sailing,' he excuses, 'Wait till she gets it on the beam a bit'!

'Really?' The Specialist murmurs.

We'll assume – laughingly – that our owner has won a cup. A very little cup, almost forgotten, probably handed over from a defunct class. By the efforts of his crew, freaks of weather, acts of God, and plain luck he has won it. The owner of the Bermudian-rigged Bentley has won overall in this case, also Class I and the Admiral's Beaker. He comes back from the top table at the race dinner with a thing the size of an elephant's foot umbrella stand. This is his hour. He has had to fill it with champagne, his tie has been cut off and his wallet feels lighter than a dead bird in an old chimney. His crew roar and neigh. At a table in the corner, Class III tore-out crews sip their bottle-between-six and chew bread.

Our owner returns with his Cup. It nestles in the palm of his hand. His crew clap politely with one hand. 'Good old Skip.' they intone.

'Shall . . . shall I fill it up lads eh?'

Then we have the family cruiser – all water bucket and boom crutch. Owners of family cruisers with 'darling' as mate command the same respect as a man doing bum con-juring tricks at a children's party. The friends who come for week-ends all want to sit on his coachroof hitching suntops. He can't see. He stands on a child and vents his repressed fury by making wild lunges with the tiller, hoping to hit Agnes.

There is always Agnes. She brings a stone of soggy pears with her like a payment of tithe and is given the owner's own deep, dark suffocatingly comfortable root berth beneath which he keeps the reef pendants, code flags, pyro-technics and a copy of a Bad Book with the cover removed. All he can do about it is to wrench the reef pendants out from under her at four a.m. and stuff them back an hour later, a routine which he keeps up throughout the passage, varied only in the matter of the article chosen each time.

You can bet an iodine sock to a cat's breakfast that sooner or later there'll be a pear core on his English Channel Middle sheet; that his wife will be offended by his tone of voice, and that Agnes will buy some art pottery which will have to be stowed in the owner's, only, own little locker.

Better to be a jolly single-hander, swaying with exhaustion and informing the world that 'It was HELL out there I tell you!' He at least can hope to have his orders obeyed.

Give me a hail

Yachtsmen show a marked reluctance to lift their voices these days. Even the race officer who jubilantly howls recalls is carried away by an enthusiasm which would be more appropriate to gun and gamebag. Apart from a distant twittering from the leeward mark our men seldom give tongue unless aided by the transistor, and even this has its draw backs. Forgetting to switch off, they treat us to some charming little domestic vignettes featuring Agnes and 'Oh-that's-right-bring-mother-into it'.

Women left stranded on the jetty with their shopping know better than to attempt a hail. There they stand, gazing out towards their ship like Sitting Bull eyeing a frontier post. Father, stretched out in a quarter berth, only becomes aware that all is not well when the sunset paints its rosy hue on the companion hatch. He is off his pad like a deterrent, scalp shuttling back and forth like a fish-fryer's shovel and oars churning the water to foam.

'I've been standing here like a fool for over an hour!' she tells him with commendable truth.

For a spine-chilling hail in the old tradition, Her Majesty's Customs Waterguard takes some beating.

'Where are you from please?' comes a bleak voice loaded with accusation.

Down below in the saloon a scene of joyless generosity is sparked off as the crew, to a man producing full bottles of stores, work desperately to reduce them to the statutory half-way mark.

'Have one on me chaps' they plead in unison turning supplicating faces to one another. I have seen men, faces twisted in bitterness around the neck of a Benedictine bottle, supping away like orphan lambs while the owner on the deck is stammering his falsetto reply.

Harbour hailing stations, built with a concrete lintel that scowls permanent disapproval, are no less ominous when they remain silent. The approaching yachtsman, trying to nose in apologetically around the breakwater with his mind still oppressed by the cheerless prose of his pilot book, has the uneasy certainty that he must be breaking at least one Port Regulation. It needs no more than the distant cackling scream of some yard foreman, who is having his boot tommed down under a shore by a first-year apprentice with a new hammer, to trigger off our owner. Certain that he is being hailed he grabs his transistor speaking trumpet.

'*Blue Grebe*, Chichester' he howls to an astonished and totally unprepared world.

The Harbour Master's nark in the watch-house is gingered into action. There is a regulation crackle from the Tannoy.

'Yacht *Blech* Yacht *Bleeb*,' he acknowledges.

'Omay od dobbit barber borb.'

Electrified by these instructions, our man goes into a tight orbit and then hastens off to anchor in the nearest prohibited area to the accompaniment of further hoots and crackles.

Old Harry, who once sang in the church choir and was thrown out the second time, is still not without a certain pride in his timbre. Tucking in his chins and clenching his fists, he delivers a series of unearthly honkings which can be loosely interpreted by listeners as they choose. I've seen him shadowed for miles by a St John's team anxious to practise Schafer's Method on him.

Club launchmen become strangely impervious to the hail. You can be clewed up and balancing on your transom while the launchman cruises to and fro, eyes glazing as he passes by. Like some monstrous bumblebee he flits from mooring to mooring with his gun'le lined with taut rumps like a rear view of Beecher's Brook. Goaded to desperation your voice rises to a coarse scream. You board the launch in an atmosphere of well-bred disgust. You then discover that your extra presence is causing your Commodore to be towed ashore on his rubber raft, looking like a large poached egg on a niggardly slice of toast.

Although Old Harry, on formal occasions or when approaching a swing bridge, may use his voice trumpet (a large enamel water jug with the bottom knocked out), he is well content to lend his unaided voice in the service of less gifted fellow yachtsmen. The owner who goes ashore for the breakfast *croissants* at eight and returns at teatime with a slack bottom lip, a paper hat and a souvenir *sabot*, has only to give one experimental hail for his dinghy when Harry is at his side sharing the sheet music. His roars will have everybody in sight safely dispatched in no time – including those who were trying to get ashore.

Startling exposures

Yachtsmen without cameras are as rare as brandy-snaps at a Darby and Joan tea-party.

Round about Michaelmas yachtsmen are busy luring each other home to look at colour transparencies. I've staggered home with my eyeballs stuck out like Barbola grapes after a fireside session of transparencies.

There you sit cradling a lap-load of cardboard windows, an interminable succession of livid bow-waves, privet-green seas and laughing helmsmen with blue necks. Each one requires a comment and the artist sits there alert to your reactions as gem after gem comes to light, he watches you with the unblinking concentration of a railway ticket collector waiting outside a corridor WC. Since every picture calls for an original remark, you need the loquacity of a fillibuster and the banality of an Xmas cracker joke writer.

You blear up at the light at another bow-wave; 'Tramping along eh!' you comment, smiling crookedly. Up comes the next shot – another bow-wave. 'Bow-wave eh!' you identify, swallowing hard.

The next is a shot up the mast, followed by another one down it. You hastily turn it right side up. 'Tricky shot' you remark.

If you are at a complete loss for words there is a master phrase that knocks 'em every time. You clear your throat; 'Hello!' you say in an alert tone, 'What did you give this one?'

You may then safely light up while he babbles away about shutter speeds and filters. It is a safe bet that any shot which went wrong and portrays high noon as a moonlight scene can be referred to as 'An interesting little study'.

The men who begin unrolling a screen as soon as the garden gate slams are the real artists. These sessions last longer because the projector has to be propped up and chairs arranged, but you can yawn in the dark and close your eyes because he will supply the patter. All you do is gasp, grunt, whistle and utter the odd congratulation such as 'Look at that sea!' and 'You've captured that one!' as if he'd gone at it with raisins and bird-lime.

There was a time when yachtsmen took 'snaps'. In those days you had a black box with a pin-hole lens and a shutter that had a clanging recoil like a towel machine. You looked into a little window, staggered around until you saw the subject and then fired. You got a picture of a man with monstrous feet and a tiny head falling over backwards and grinning serenely.

You could search the creeks and harbours with a bucket and riddle but you'd never find the camera-less yachtsman nowadays. The man without that little leather pod hung round his neck is as rare as brandy-snaps at a Darby and Joan tea-party.

You see them lurching around, peering through viewfinders, gathering in great ripe clusters at mastheads, like hibernating bats, sidling slyly around fish-markets and striding backwards off quays in search of better composition.

I've seen yachts flash past with the lee rail loaded with head-down photographers fiercely capturing the bow-wave which will ultimately appear as a turgid little ripple like the neck-line of a hired tail suit. Camera mechanics spend a great deal of their working year winkling bow-waves out of cameras.

The movie man has the rest of them wrapped up and stacked when it comes to expertise. 'We'll have Blanch walking down the side-deck!' he orders, winding his clockwork. This breath-taking sequence will lull his teeth-gritting guests for winters to come. None of these shots last more than a split second and the disjointed nightmare of grinning, waving, gesturing, silent figures interspersed with boats which go shuddering across the steeply heeled horizon creates an abstract fantasia which would make the ravings of an opium-eater seem like a Mable Lucy Atwell rag book.

In the good old black-and-white days, when a man could shut himself in the fo'c'sle and play with his negatives, life was simple. Give him a bottle of hypo and a cupboard under the stairs in which he could fumble crash and curse, and he was yours for life. On a clear night the racket of amateurs in cupboards mixing fix and agitating their spools sounded like a posse of untipped dustmen booting lids around an alley.

Colour film has struck a rude blow at the peace-loving. Let Old Harry appear through the forehatch with his cap off revealing his two-tone scalp, and they're at him with their light-meters like paupers rallying round a Maundy gift. Diagnosed as 'a 50th at F8', I've seen that man surreptitiously examining his tongue for days after.

Leaning on a butt

Notes on winter workers – and their advisers

Just put hammer to boat, and instantly up comes every slack-time Charlie, every Saturday Admiral and every ten-thumbs who ever assembled a crate and threw away the kit.

How is it that they can choose the exact moment when they are the least welcome? Why do they arrive just when there's something to be hidden? You may be canvasing a deck. It's all gone on flat save for one stout wrinkle which you've chased all over the deck and finally cornered by the forehatch coaming. Just as you're belting it flat and peppering it with tacks you become conscious of old needle-nose peering over your shoulder.

'Pity!' he says with triumph.

Mankind is divided equally into two opposing factions – those who say you should wet the canvas before stretching it and the dry-at-all-costs men. Our foredeck has more bumps than a clock golf course, and showing clearly under the paint are the words 'Batcher's Best Calf Meal'. Wet or dry it has as much stretch as a tin roof. Whichever method you choose you'll be wrong.

Take splicing wire. There you are, deep in a thicket of bristling strands which are all trying to get up your nose at the same time, and all home and dry save for an unaccountable extra strand which wasn't there a minute ago. Just as you poke it out of sight and reach for some parcelling, up comes razor-beak and gives a bewildered little laugh.

'Well that's something I've learnt,' he says nastily, 'I've never seen that tuck done before!' You drive the spike deep into your shuddering flesh and scream a foul oath.

I've seen little men trying to hide their splices with all their fingers and thumbs arranged over kinked turns and strange tucks as if they were playing a piccolo. Just let me get a serving on and I can laugh at them.

Now I am not a careful craftsman. I can slam a cool dump and tar a tingle with the best of them but I am not one of these bib-and-brace, poor-man's-Chippendale artists who can't cut a finger without first using a set-square. I rub sawdust into my dove-tails and what paint won't cure I put my cap over, but for all this I pride myself on work that stands the test of time.

There's Old Harry, too. He uses a seven pound claw-headed screwdriver swung from the shoulder, and to see him caulking a deck is as pretty a sight as could be wished for. He looks like a serf hoeing sideways in one of those medieval prints in a history book. All he needs is wool boots and a home-spun gym-slip.

I've seen him stuffing seams with the desperate energy of a man packing a weekend case whilst the taxi waits at the door. Admittedly those seams look as if the swallows were nesting there, but a razor soon takes care of that. People keep well clear of Harry and his hammer. I've seen a seam which contained half a club tie, a finger-stall, two toe-caps and something odd in wool.

It's the advice we can't stomach. Just as the awful realization that you've cut a short end a quarter inch shy is settling upon you, you feel a blast of hot breath down your neck – your fingers contract fiercely on the knob of red lead putty.

'It's a job you just can't hurry!' he comments. (If I had more time on my hands than the Wandering Jew my butts would still fit like a mail order overcoat). His eyes go wandering over to a graving piece that looks like a stop-cock lid, and on to the grinning seams and pouting scarphs. All you can do is lean on the butt and clap your cap over the scarph, and just wait wagging your head from side to side to distract him from the graving piece the while.

Winter work on our mobile mussel-bed consists mainly of rot-doctoring and oakum-poking, but we have the occasional tear-out of the accommodation aimed at improving the lay-out, although a slab of gun-cotton is the only practical answer there. We do get a chance to see behind the saloon panelling, of course, and Harry dabs around with Cuprinol at anything within reach like an army doctor who's just discovered gentian violet. Harry fancies himself as a crusader against dry-rot, a sort of Pasteur-in-gumboots. Give him a cathedral and a bucket of copper napthalate and you'd never see him again.

This preoccupation has its rewards. There was a time when a poker-snout came around to watch me remove a split strake. I heaved. 'You never know what you'll see behind the planking in an old boat do you,' he said, smiling with half his mouth only. The plank came away and revealed Old Harry's rudimentary features framed in the gap . . . he looked like the ghost of Hamlet's father looking through a letter box . . .

That man never really recovered.

A bit o' science

With the exception of our parallel rules which stumble around the chart with the slack-knee'd shuffle of a ferryboat passenger carrying tea, our sole scientific instrument is the compass. It lives in a battered brass mosque

with outhouses, and stands on a plinth like a bust of Plato, square in the way of anyone making for aft. Clap a cloth cap on it and you'd think you had the lodger out for the day.

With the top off, you can stand your mug on it in safety and, by leaving the spoon in, a bearing can be taken, which is science at its best.

We favour the older type of compass. Those plastic blisters sprouting from sinister little black bowls look as if a hot fomentation would not be inappropriate. By comparison with our card, which has more scrollwork, arabesques and fleurs-de-lis than a postal school diploma, these are so sparsely marked that it's like trying to steer by pianola music.

Let me see the whole card laid out before me like a school dinner, bobbing in its bubbling aquarium, yellow as convent seed cake and pointing faithfully to Old Harry's cutlass. We do have a little deviation. If you took that card out of its bowl, it would follow you around the deck snapping at the fasteners on your braces, but since Old Harry renounces deviation with spirit and refuses to believe in variation, our courses are either frighteningly accurate or else we get to visit a lot of new places. This is of less importance than it might be if our chart were readable. Before now we've rounded a non-existent headland of cocoa and sounded our way cautiously over a shoal of egg.

Illumination of the bowl by night is important. Those little plastic pickle-jars have a pinpoint of light illuminating one figure at a time. They're like those intimate little restaurants, where a pool of rosy light reveals your grubby cuffs and leaves you groping in Stygian blackness for your fish-fork.

With ours it's like peering into a blast furnace when both lamps are on. To light them you take the mosque below, then you shut the doors and bring it on deck. The lights go out. The trick lies in shuffling the mosque along the deck then, waiting one's chance, clap it smartly over the compass. I've seen it belching smoke and flame like an anniversary dinner, hot enough to spit at and bathing Old Harry in an unearthly radiance. He looked like the prow of a war canoe.

'Dew pong'

Going foreign? Language should present no difficulty – if in doubt, point!

It's all right for us because Harry speaks the language. 'Blong,' he says, slowly and deliberately. Then, holding up a couple of fingers like earthy carrots and pursing up his moustache, 'doo.'

'Oh, two white wines, eh.' Madame says.

We would get that even if we wanted paregoric because *vin blanc* and the British are bracketed.

The lure of language takes more Britons to France than flies to wet paint and they have a particular accent for speaking French, slightly high and nasal. If they don't know a word of the language they just beam and nod like a shop window Father Christmas, and come in with a musical *bon* like a slack string on a double bass every time there's a gap in the flow.

Phrase books are no help. I once wanted to find the Bureau-de-something-or-other, worked it out in the book, memorized the noises and waited for a passer-by. I found one, let him have it, waited confidently. He told me in rapid French and left me rocking on my heels. I never got there.

Take shopping for the ship. 'Pah' they say emphatically,

pointing at the bread. Or by way of variation, 'dew pong, pon, pain.' That they ever get it is a lasting tribute to French versatility. The active will trot miles in the early morning in order to buy *croissants* which is pronounced with variations from 'crrresong' to what sounds something like 'creosote.' Breakfast on these occasions is at a quarter past eleven.

There's one type of sound British yachtsman who can be relied upon to send the French yelping for cover. This is the fellow with the 'French accent'. He pokes his snout in the air pursed up like a baying hound and gives out with a brand of French you could scrape off the ceiling.

In a tone, faint to the point of exhaustion, he groans, flutes and purrs along, producing every vowel sound from a dialling tone to nanny blowing the candle out. He makes *Croix de Guerre* sound like a dog-fight and *petit pois* as if he'd smelt something.

Father, who understands about foreign foods, knows of a 'nice little table wine' and wanders off alone to buy it (which is why the British stick to white). He comes back with a bottle of red so dry you could blow it out in dust. It draws in your cheeks like a deflated whoopee cushion.

No voyage is right without 'The Meal.' Every man becomes a pint-size gourmet, even though he doesn't know beans on toast from a hole in the wall. He must go through with it, and build up a liver like a bicycle saddle, and climb down an iron ladder at midnight, and burp alarmingly in the hushed yacht basin so that his wife can give him a spirited blast from the saloon skylight.

Every summer the woolly hordes set out across Channel – each man a Captain Cook in sand-shoes. More and more new yachtsmen hurl themselves across the Channel each year. They spill out from the Wight and in the course of time hit the sluicing tides off Barfleur and spend a grisly night zooming back and forth off the Cherbourg peninsular, trying to hit the hole in the breakwater like Dad trying to find the keyhole after a Regimental Reunion.

They make it at dawn and, grey-faced Magellans triumphant in the joyless British tradition, they enter the yacht basin, breaching the mesh of fishing lines on the mole which is France's last line of defence.

The atmosphere of foreign places starts soon after leaving the Nab, when father remarks that it might be an idea to have a *tas* of the old *thé*. Tension mounts until, half-way there, someone gets out the French flag ('the trickler' as we British call it) and flies it from the cross-trees. If it doesn't turn out to be the Dutch one, which it often does because Dad never can remember which way the stripes go. A typically foreign arrangement this we feel. Anyway if it's not right it will be a comfort and a reassurance to the French who like flags, though it is faintly embarrassing to father who feels as if he was wearing a paper hat.

The sense of sin which accompanies visits to foreign parts adds to the lark. There was never so desperate a rogue as our tight-lipped yachtsman sidling into the Bureau de Change to buy an illegal quid's worth of francs, and the eye-rolling and winking that goes into his account of a night ashore makes a Left Bank roué look like Little Dorrit. (He was wheeled twice round the floor by a motherly dance-hostess and spilt his Pernod down his club tie).

We won't miss a chance to sit at a table in the street for a glass of 'vinn blong' even if an onshore gale has our club ties cracking like stock-whips and 'darling' has her souvenir scarf wrapped round her neck like a lagged stove pipe. We never find the *family* places though. It's either the joint with the potted trees where *l'addition* whips the smirk of your face as if you'd been garrotted, or it's a quaint fisherman's *bistro* where you get nobbled by an old man in a leather coat who shows you a scar and smokes all your Players.

There are yachtsmen who do their damnedest to get mistaken for Frenchmen and rush out to buy berets. They get them a size too big, giving the effect of a man unaccountably wearing a hassock. The alternative is one of those little peaked caps that look deep-sea on a Frenchman and make an Englishman look like a night club tout.

The man who thinks he's got to haggle for everything he

buys is nearly extinct among yachtsmen. A breed of French shop assistants grew up and flattened them. This breed has heavy lidded eyes and a near-Oxford accent that, combined with a gift for pricing your pants as you stand, sends our merchant adventurers scuttling out clutching a souvenir ink stand made of shells and glad to escape.

Then there's always somebody who has a firm distrust of the foreigner and believes that an elephant gun should be carried anywhere south of Dover. He still has a firm belief that English is intelligible to anyone as long as you shout.

Since a sense of sin pervades the whole affair, it's fitting that these Marco Polonecks should land in the blue serge lap of HM Customs when they get home. Even if they have never smuggled anything worse than a pair of plastic braces, everyone has theories of how they *could* smuggle – they don't, but they like to feel that they might.

Picture the saloon with 'him' aboard.

All are gathered there, affecting an air of nonchalance that's as convincing as the cardboard skull in High School Hamlet. Adam's apples shoot up and down like slide-valves, and lips are moistened with the doleful deliberation of cows at a salt-lick. The officer cracks a mild and official joke at which everybody, released from tension, laughs too long and too shrilly.

It is a dangerous hour. The patient officer, anxious to let them down as gently as the rules will allow, plays out the game to its hilarious end. His finger moves over the form as the adventurers fill it in with shaky, purposeful strokes, entering a suspiciously exact two hundred cigarettes in the cigar column and hoping that 'part bot wine' will cover the Vermouth.

'Now is there anything else *at all*?' he asks, slowly and distinctly, allowing a long and terrible pause. 'Think *carefully*.' This is the moment of truth. Silence save for stertorous breathing and swallowing.

A very long silence. Then ... Captain Kidd with the plastic braces cracks up and confesses. Honour is saved.